The
Elements

A Widowhood

Kat Lister

ICON

This edition published in the UK in 2022
by Icon Books Ltd, Omnibus Business Centre,
39–41 North Road, London N7 9DP
email: info@iconbooks.com
www.iconbooks.com

Previously published in the UK in 2021 by Icon Books Ltd

Sold in the UK, Europe and Asia
by Faber & Faber Ltd, Bloomsbury House,
74–77 Great Russell Street,
London WC1B 3DA or their agents

Distributed in the UK, Europe and Asia
by Grantham Book Services,
Trent Road, Grantham NG31 7XQ

Distributed in Australia and New Zealand
by Allen & Unwin Pty Ltd,
PO Box 8500, 83 Alexander Street,
Crows Nest, NSW 2065

Distributed in South Africa
by Jonathan Ball, Office B4, The District,
41 Sir Lowry Road, Woodstock 7925

Distributed in India by Penguin Books India,
7th Floor, Infinity Tower – C, DLF Cyber City,
Gurgaon 122002, Haryana

ISBN: 978-178578-795-9

Typeset in Bembo by Marie Doherty

Printed and bound in Great Britain
by Clays Ltd, Elcograf S.p.A.

Praise for *The Elements*

'Powerful, humane and deeply affecting, Lister's wise and truthful writing makes this essential reading for anyone touched, and utterly confused, by grief.'
Sali Hughes

'Strikingly honest'
Sarah Ditum, *The Times*

'A stunning and immersive examination of grief; of making a new future; the body as a site of "wrongness" and "re-entry" after bereavement ... it veers from melancholy to rage and joy.'
Sinéad Gleeson

'The must-read memoir. A moving, bruising and meditative memoir and love story ... Beautifully written, *The Elements* will strike a chord with anyone who's been touched by grief.'
Sarra Manning, *Red* **magazine**

'A staggering book. Kat writes with such hypnotic lyricism.'
Terri White

'It is not just one of the most beautiful books I've ever read, exploring grief through the elements of the cosmos, it is the only book I've read that has made me feel less alone. A must read even if it's not your own experience.'
Poorna Bell

'It knocked me for six: the honesty in it, the frankness, the detail, the research, the feeling, and such stunning writing ... it's not just about losing someone. It's about rebuilding.'
Jude Rogers

'The writing will make you stop to catch your breath, it's hopeful in ways you won't expect at all, and the smallest moments will break your heart.'
Sian Meades-Williams

'It is lyrical. It is wise. It is physical in its longing ... Destined to become a classic. *The Elements* is a gift; not so much a map but a compass, to a landscape we long not to visit but many of us do.'
Sam Baker

'Brilliant, beautiful, moving.'
The Anchoress

'Such a searingly honest book that will stop you cold with its beauty. Kat's unique voice and perspective on death, love and womanhood really get under your skin. This is a book about grief but it's also about finding a sense of self after a deep loss, and hoping above everything for something wonderful that feels very much like joy.'
Tigers Are Better Looking

For Pat Long

My life is not this steeply sloping hour
Through which you see me hasten on.
I am a tree standing before my background
I am but one of many of my mouths
The one that closes before all of them.

I am the rest between two notes
That harmonize only reluctantly:
For death wants to become the loudest tone—

But in the dark interval they reconcile
Tremblingly, and get along.
    And the beauty of the song goes on.

— Rainer Maria Rilke, *The Book of Hours*, 1905

ABOUT THE AUTHOR

Kat Lister is a writer and editor based in London. Beginning her career as a music journalist at the *NME*, she has gone on to write widely for publications including *Vice*, the *Guardian*, *Marie Claire*, *Vogue* and the *Feminist Times*, where she was appointed Contributing Editor. In 2017, she joined the editorial team at *The Pool*, becoming a freelance features and news editor until its demise in 2019. Since her husband's death in 2018, she has focused on investigating her experience of grief, writing widely circulated essays and features for *The Sunday Times Magazine*, *Sunday Times Style* and *The Observer Magazine*.

CONTENTS

INTRODUCTION

Have you ever watched a great cloud smudge like chalk into the faraway horizon? Wispy tails of precipitation that streak down and down towards the earth in vertical lines. A translucent curtain of dangling tentacles, each one evaporating from liquid to vapour before it even has time to reach solid ground.

Some call it *the jellyfish of the skies*.

I call it grief.

I last saw this meteorological curiosity in the spring of 2019, ten months after my husband died. I was standing on a rooftop car park in south-east London, looking out across the railway tracks, when my eyes were drawn to the dove-grey threads that marbled the sharp nib of the Shard in the distance, and for a brief moment I lost myself to these ghostly squiggles, these disintegrating fingertips, reflecting all the wraith-like movements I felt inside. There was something about this shapeshifting skyline that mirrored the nebulous outlines of my own widowhood, such as they were on that Saturday afternoon, dripping and blotting, curving and streaking, before evaporating into gas – a vanishing act that tricked the senses because it wasn't disappearing at all, it was actually remaking itself from one state into another.

This car park epiphany wasn't the first time I had stepped into nature in order to delve into my grief. When my life upended in 2018, I reached outwards for the elements – fire, water, earth and air – because they helped me to understand the wild sensations I felt inside. The burning flames that needled across my skin and the implacable waves that crashed beneath it. The entwining roots that spread around my limbs and the bracing wind that whipped upwards and through me, tangling my hair.

These elements weren't always easy to carry. In the early days of my grief, I would walk them around the perimeter of my local park, often in the rain, reassured by the gentle spots that pattered against the canopy of my umbrella. At night, I would stack up splinters of kindling inside my living room stove and watch a flickering of mustard and apricot pop and crackle into a blaze of enraged ruby flames.

In the astral light at 3am, during the first winter of my grief, it was the sound of the wind through the leaves of a silver birch tree in my garden that gave me comfort and reassurance as I struggled to sleep. Roots and branches. Cycles and movement. The rustling of a world outside my window. When my home became a time capsule to what had been lost, I often found myself wandering from room to room in the early hours of the morning, willing my husband to speak as I reached for his sweater and smothered my face into its bobbled sleeves.

I saw him everywhere. Amongst his battered John Le Carré books neatly arranged on the bookshelf. Between the cans of Guinness rammed at the back of our fridge. A toothbrush casually discarded by the sink. In his laundry – worn socks, treasured shirts, faded jeans – randomly intertwined with mine.

A scattering of unremarkable objects that served to document the past like some kind of spectral crime scene: exhibits of a life shared and a life lost. Strewn buoys that ringed my drifting grief raft in this house we lived in, the house we loved, now a strange, unbearably quiet and dark expanse.

My story begins here, days after my husband died in his hospice bed – sleepwalking through the debris of cataclysmic loss. It was a foreign land occupied by shadows and past lives. A time when wakefulness finally succumbed to half-dreaming visions and invading memories. For it was during these nocturnal hours that my husband's gentle presence seemed to unfurl. In this hypnagogic state, I was convinced that he had briefly returned to me, as if a celestial pathway could somehow reunite us between two disparate worlds. And maybe I was right, perhaps it could, albeit briefly. But magic is a transient illusion. All spells eventually break. Weeks turn to months, seasons evolve, the earth silently spins. I felt the oscillations rippling inside me, reverberations that signalled renewal. *Grief cannot hold you here*, they thrummed. But these sensations also betrayed the past, initiating a forwards and backwards motion that gradually pulled me away from the 35-year-old woman I recognised – the woman I had been.

I yearned for movement, I feared letting go. It was here, in this paradoxical moment, that death splintered me in two, creating dual identities, dancing and sparring, in darkness and light.

In the twelve months after my husband died of a glioblastoma brain tumour, many people asked me how it felt: to love, to grieve, to lose. Like a curious head poked through the shattered windshield of a concertinaed car wreck, this is akin to asking the slumped driver inside to point at a body part and show bystanders where it hurts. Pain is essential, it helps us identify our injuries and protect ourselves from any further harm, but it can also be difficult to quantify. There is no Richter scale for loss, no abacus that can calculate your daily progress as you hurtle from one extreme emotion to the next. There is simply no way to monitor your own heart's rhythms when the one it was tied to stops beating.

I began writing in the winter of 2018 to confront the ugly facets of my grief, but I continued writing to try to co-opt them. It was the only way I could control what was happening inside me, the elemental changes that seemed to transform me from solid to liquid to gas, a transmutation that sometimes occurred in a single day as I went about my everyday tasks: wheeling a trolley through the supermarket aisle, rushing down an underground escalator to get to work, waiting in line at my local cafe to buy a takeaway coffee.

No one warned me about the power grief can wield over your subconscious, the way it ruthlessly inhabits and subverts you. In the immediate aftermath of my husband's death, I struggled to locate him amid the debris; yet over time this quest ricocheted inward, a pursuit no longer focused on the absence around me, but the gaping chasm within. Perhaps that's why I turned to widowed writers, scientific researchers and academic books to soothe the judgemental voice in my head that told me I was doing it wrong, grieving badly. I was looking for answers. I sought reassurance in the things I had never been told.

On a rainy afternoon, surrounded by medical books in London's Wellcome Library, I uncovered tales of Native American women, widows of the Hopi Tribe in north-western Arizona, who have been known to experience spontaneous hallucinations of their dead husbands as a symptom of unresolved grief. I read stories of dolphins carrying their dead loved ones for days, refusing to eat or sleep, and elephants that returned, again and again, to the carcasses of their dead companions. I found strange comfort in the idea of 'grieving geese' who have been known to withdraw socially and lose weight after the loss of their mate.

Drowning in legal paperwork – bureaucratic obligations that seemed to homogenise and normalise his death – I took refuge in fairy stories as a way to escape. Faraway kingdoms that lassoed me away from reality. Enchanted spirit-lands inhabited by talking rivers, armless maidens and howling she-wolves. A beast that growls because he cannot speak. A frail white rose smeared with blood. Gothic prose that weaved wild worlds like vast spiders' webs around me. I later recognised that these stories didn't lasso me away from reality at all. Angela Carter once described fairy tales as 'the science fiction of the past'. She called them 'the land of bears and shooting stars'. Perhaps that's why I dived into them so fervidly. When my life crossed over into make-believe, it was fantasy that recreated what I'd lost, feral allegories that brought me back to my love, and back to the shock. The more I read, the more I understood: these strange fables repeatedly sprung from death, the only narrative I could relate to as I filled out funeral paperwork in permanent black ink. And so, I cast myself as the armless maiden who lay at the foot of a nursing bed. As the white rose smeared with blood. The she-wolf that howled as the morphine carried him away, light years away, to that far-off land of bears and shooting stars.

And yet, the real-life tale of the 35-year-old widow – the one who resides in south-east London? That was harder to find. I desperately searched for her amongst the bookshelves, a benevolent daemon that might be hiding in the spaces between words. She wasn't there. Struggling to find a narrative that matched my crippling dysmorphia, I did the only thing I could: I wrote. When speech failed me, language danced frantically inside. Filling notepads and diaries, tapping into note apps, scribbling onto random serviettes and graffitiing across discarded envelopes, I narrated my own story. Scared of forgetting, I squirrelled away scraps of memories around my house, mysterious clues left by one version of myself for another to find. In the months that followed, I became a walking anachronism, mimicking everyday interactions as I internally conversed with the husband I had lost. Grief can split a person into multiple forms and sometimes they can communicate through time. In many ways, this book is a testament to this shapeshifting personality: wife and widow, witness and reporter. Who I was, and who I'm yet to be.

If the goal is to achieve some kind of profound transformation, then I suppose that grief turned me into a quester of sorts. My story seemed to correlate with the surreal bedtime tales that had captivated my imagination as a child: Alice through the looking-glass, Dorothy and her slippers, Lucy and a dusty wardrobe that leads into Narnia. Characters who journeyed to far-flung lands in order to capture something precious before finally returning home. My yellow brick road took me from the rugged peaks of Andalucía to the tempestuous waters of Mexico's Pacific coast. As winter softened into spring, and my first complete year without the man I married passed, I wandered further into the outdoors, drawn to wild woods and kaleidoscopic skies. Meandering under towering elm trees and rustling leaves, I felt the ground beneath me, I found the words inside me – and, opening a blank notebook, I began to write.

My experience of widowhood might be unique to me, but considered in this context of far-flung lands, I hope that it has something universal to say about departure and return. The cryptic loop that brings us back to ourselves. Haven't we all been thrown into the metaphorical woods at some point in our lives? Haven't we all tried to retrieve something intangible beneath those elm trees – a displaced feeling, a failed relationship, a younger incarnation, even – despite everything we've seen and everything we know? Find me someone who hasn't traipsed aimlessly over the past in order to find a reflection they recognise, a future to strive for, a narrative that fits. Are you still searching? So am I – and here's my proof. Burn the maps. This is loss. A state of unbeing propelled by hope: a wild and radical feeling that can prevail, even in the depths of trauma and despair.

With this in mind, perhaps my story can be yours, too, because if my first year of mourning has taught me anything it's that the elements are all around us. Sooner or later, if we open ourselves up to possibility, we all have something to lose. And whilst I hope my story reaches out to any young widow who, like me, has desperately searched for herself amongst the bookshelves, I also want to speak to anyone who's ever lost something significant in their lives. Something they believed in, something they took a chance on, something they loved. A loss so estranging, it harkens back to the word *loss*'s Germanic origins – *to loosen, divide, cut apart*.

Maybe death is the greatest disrupter of them all: a loss so extreme that any semblance of *life after* is forever shaped by it. That doesn't mean the chances of reconfiguring yourself are any less possible. During my first year of widowhood, I watched my former life dissolve and effervesce, transforming from one substance to another and sometimes back again. Don't let my published words fool you with their finality. We are all chemical reactions. The elements are within me, too. Even now, as I write this, I am transforming.

Into what, exactly? I'm still trying to figure that one out. Scientists call the physical process of post-trauma repair 'wound healing', but the miraculous regrowth is never quite the same. Scars remain in faithfulness to tell their story. Words have helped me to tell mine. Like clusters of incandescent stars, they led me out of the dark woods.

In the astral light at 3am, they kept me alive.

Part I

FIRE

Ashes denote that fire was;
Respect the grayest pile
For the departed creature's sake
That hovered there awhile.

Fire exists the first in light,
And then consolidates,—
Only the chemist can disclose
Into what carbonates.

— Emily Dickinson, 'Ashes denote that Fire was',
Poem 1063, c.1886–96

ONE

In a moment of anguish, perhaps madness, I licked the ashes from my fingertips and swallowed him down. He tasted of embers. Memories of childhood bonfire nights that danced on the tip of my tongue. The firm squeeze of my father's hand as the crackle and hiss of a shooting firework surrendered to a *bang-bang-bang* of pyrotechnic stars. Flashes of brilliance that rocketed across the sky. An explosion, a jolt, then stillness. The taste of him brought me back here, back to the fire and the blast and the dust. Here, where sulphurous plumes permeated the air, enveloping me in the dark, my neck craned upwards, squinting for a horizon that had momentarily disappeared.

'We view our memories as sacred,' my husband wrote in 2017, meditating on the brain tumour that would take his life the following year. 'They make up the autobiographical map that helps us navigate the present day.' His words guided me on the day I scattered his ashes. On a crisp autumn morning in 2018, past and present blurred. Like the reassuring squeeze of my father's hand when I was a child, glimmers of my husband's sage wisdom helped me to complete my widowly duty on the banks of the River Thames. I reached into the wicker casket and dipped my palm inside, gently caressing him back and forth; once whole, now multitudinous, like millions of indistinguishable grains of sand.

He had asked to be scattered in Richmond-upon-Thames, at the bend of the river where we had picnicked on an early date in 2009. It was a characteristically romantic idea, but one that required a bit of practical planning to see it through. Questions needed to be asked, nautical information ascertained, which is what brought me to the water's edge days after his death, standing bewildered on a Thames-side walkway discussing tide times with an apathetic boatman chewing gum. The rental would cost me £8 an hour, I was informed, as he scribbled his number on a scrap of paper. An arrangement was made, a time-slot decided. My mum picked us up in her Volkswagen Polo. What had originated as a romantic dying wish suddenly felt like a logistical test that I would either pass or fail to complete.

I placed the container of ashes in the backseat of the car, strapped myself into the seat beside them and listened to the mellow burble of Radio 4 as we drove. When I closed my eyes and tried to remember our picnic a decade earlier, something stirred. The sensation of damp grass between my toes. The touch of his fingers as they traced their way across the nape of my neck. Limbs and eyes and mouths on skin.

Anticipation.

I wasn't expecting to see him that day. Our first date had occurred the previous evening, involving a priceless incident with a shot of black pepper vodka. I had brought him to my favourite Polish restaurant in Shepherd's Bush. I watched him – half-enthusiastically, half-trepidatiously – plunge his fork into a plate of pickled herring and sauerkraut, and, between slurps of beetroot soup, I chronicled my mother's arduous journey from Gdańsk to London in the late 1950s. He listened attentively, leaning in to butterfly-catch every word. He always listened this way and sometimes, when he replied, I heard cosmic symphonies.

You can't always pinpoint a feeling, but I'm pretty sure our opening sonata began that evening over a midnight plate of plum pierogi on Goldhawk Road. Against the soft patter of April showers, he began to unfurl, a sequence of movements that opened numerous doors to spectacular worlds. Arvo Pärt's *Cantus in Memoriam Benjamin Britten*. The dusky tones of the British Post-Impressionist Walter Sickert. Our shared appreciation of Larry David. The unparalleled brilliance of all-you-can-eat dim sum. Then – *wham!* – the table between us shook. Interrupted by a cajoling babcia who had slammed her extensive vodka menu down, the conversation immediately diverted to neat liquor, but which one? His index finger zig-zagged down the list of flavours – plum, cherry, honey, bison grass – until it lingered at a danger zone marked pepper, his one eyebrow raised.

'Don't go there,' I warned.

'Why not?' he asked.

'I just wouldn't.'

'You wouldn't?'

He did. Twelve hours later, I was walking home from the supermarket when my mobile pinged. He'd made it out the other side, he quipped, and this weather was too good to miss.

'Meet me in Richmond?'

On a sunny September morning, a decade after we lay tipsy and outstretched on the riverbed grass, my best friend Andy rowed a boat out whilst I cradled my husband tightly between my knees. With every rock of the skiff, I held on tighter to the casket, marvelling at the weight of him, the density he had left behind. No one had warned me about this, I thought to myself, as the boat's oars skimmed the water. This gravitational pull, the earthy tangibility of death. With every handful I released, he rippled and swirled. I watched him swell and billow beneath the surface. Microscopic clusters of phosphates and minerals that danced and dispersed like sparkling stardust trails.

That's the thing about ashes. They linger amongst us, just like sulphurous plumes and evocative childhood memories, finding lifelines you never knew existed. Quite literally, in my case. As I sprinkled him onto the water, powdered flecks of him carried away with the breeze, dispersing through my hair and settling on my skin. They clung to the bodily tributaries that forked across the palms of my hands, finding a way into the contours and creases. Using the sleeve of my T-shirt, I wiped away the pepper-pot dust that coated the screen of my iPhone. And when I reached inside the top pocket of my dungarees for a scrap of tissue, I found him there too. Perhaps this explains my visceral urge to taste the ashes that day. In the chasm of grief, this was no longer a rational world. Standing in a pub toilet with his remnants under my fingernails, anguish turned to horror. Where should they go? *From fingertips to mouth*, a primal voice replied. Then I turned on the basin taps and watched the rest of him drain away.

In order to understand the woman who licked her ashen fingers like they were sherbet straws, we need to go back, right back, to when the tectonic plates shifted. Nine years ago, on a Sunday evening in 2012, my life changed irreparably. Roughly a week after my husband's 35th birthday, a year before we married, he blacked out on his kitchen floor waiting for the kettle to boil. We were living in separate ends of London at the time, so when he called me at 10pm to tell me that he'd woken with bruises scattered down one side of his face and torso, that he was going to run a bath, and that he really didn't think a hospital dash would be necessary, I urged him to call a taxi. True to form, he said he *absolutely would* and jumped on the bus. A rudimentary CT scan in an east London Accident & Emergency department revealed that for the length of our three-year relationship, a tumour had been steadily growing in the right side of his brain. It was the size of a lemon, we were later told, and a neurosurgeon would need to operate immediately in order to diagnose its type and grade.

It's hard to do it, even now. Stand on the charred ground and look down. I'm giving it a go for the sake of the story, but I'm not sure that it's possible to rake over the past and examine what happened without neatening it a little, or smoothing over the rough surface in some way. I can squish the main details into a couple of paragraphs, but it doesn't give you the messy bits I have tried to block out, and it is the messy bits that I need to confront. The misshapen parts that I'm tempted to kick away because they complicate the narrative and expose the flaws. Or maybe they expose my flaws, maybe it's that. The truth is that my naivety on that night still haunts me because I couldn't foresee it – the brain tumour – and a part of me still believes that if I had, it might not have happened at all. Which sounds implausible but, then again, so is what happened next.

Between his midnight bus trip and the 2am CT scan on a busy A&E ward, I fell asleep at home waiting for news. I was convinced that he had simply sleepwalked during an afternoon nap and walked into his bookshelf. He did that fairly regularly. He also dropped his keys a lot – so much so that I ribbed him for it. It wasn't until I woke up at 7.30am that I saw a voicemail on my iPhone screen and listened to his three-minute message telling me that they had found a large mass in his brain and that he had been admitted for further tests. I placed the mobile phone carefully on my bedside table and, kneeling on my bed, smacked my hand repeatedly against my forehead – rapid, sharp blows that came at me again and again, as if my arm belonged to someone else entirely. Even now, I can feel the slaps, the burning sensation it left on my skin, a primal attempt to jolt me out of what was happening, and an ineffectual one, because all it left me with was the present. A fire that was raging between my temples.

Memory can be a unreliable resource, especially in times of trauma, but I can recall the afternoon we were first introduced to the words 'glioblastoma multiforme' with the same precision as the grocery list I scribbled down on a Post-It note this morning. I can still see my husband reaching into a trouser pocket for his mobile and Googling the words as we waited for a copy of his scans in a consulting room at Homerton

University Hospital. I can picture his face as he swiped through the Wikipedia page whilst I pleaded with him to stop. I can hear the loud *whoosh* of the automatic sliding doors as we left in silence. I can remember the cold blast of air and the smack of heavy rain on the tarmac outside the main entrance. And I can feel my legs buckling underneath me, followed by the dull sensation of knees hitting concrete as I concertinaed to the floor. It was only when my husband hoisted me back to my feet that I realised that the loud wails I could hear across the car park were actually my own.

A steroid was prescribed, dexamethasone, to reduce the swelling. This wasn't a treatment, we were informed, but a way to manage symptoms, prevent further seizures, mellow that crude sound *tumour* with a soft pedal approach. But the hammer mechanism kept doggedly on, and the pills made him hyperactive and awake. I pounded the pavements to work each morning in an absent daze. My husband attended a brain exhibition in central London. Devouring a plate of fish and chips later that evening, he told me about a Bronze Age skull he'd discovered in the cutting section, drilled with four burr holes.

I avoided the fruit aisle in our local supermarket.

He emailed me citrus jokes.

The lemon-sized tumour kept growing.

Weeks later, he was urgently wheeled into a basement operating room at the National Hospital for Neurology and Neurosurgery in London. As he lay on the operating table, I was packing boxes and moving us into our first home together: bubble-wrapping crockery, ornaments and glassware as his neurosurgeon resected, welded and stitched for twelve straight hours across the other side of town. In the early hours of the evening, I sat on a plastic seat outside his recovery room and waited for news as the hot drinks vending machine vibrated and whirred from the other end of the corridor. There was a faint smell of citrus in the air, or maybe it was just the hospital disinfectant spray, but when my husband called out my name, the delirium was instantly quelled. The bulk tumour had been excised, we were told. His mother and I watched him take exhilarated sips of milky tea through a straw and I stroked his hand as he proclaimed that *this was the best cup of tea he had ever tasted*. Somewhere between those slurps we stepped over the borderline between our past and future lives without even realising it, a shift so imperceptible that it was lost in the euphoria of his widening smile, in this diaphanous moment between recovery bays. When the results of his biopsy came through a week later we were told that they'd removed a Grade 2 oligoastrocytoma, a 'mixed glioma' tumour that is made up of a variety of different glial cells that makes its behaviour difficult to predict. In layman's terms, it was complicated, and this diagnosis would never be a stable one – but for now, at least, his condition was under control.

Emily Dickinson once described hope as a 'strange invention'. I think I understand what she meant. The idea that hope is something that is imagined and willed and constructed into existence. I welded the clunky parts – the confusing scans, the lengthy hospital appointments, the *Let's not go there just yet* evasive replies – and I fused them together with the heat of my own ignorance. I softened them and sculpted them without ever asking his doctors the one question that pulsed through me day after day: *But when will he die?* Although I was unaware of it at the time, my husband's diagnosis marked a point where I began to construct stories in order to avoid what was happening. The frightening reality that our lives were now moulded around a tumour that I couldn't see nor fully understand. On the morning of my husband's first appointment at the National Hospital for Neurology and Neurosurgery, he dressed in a suit and tie, carefully writing down notes in a writing pad, and when his neurosurgeon circled his capped biro around the globular white-and-grey mass that had invaded the right-hand side of his brain, I burst into tears. The neurosurgeon looked at me, surprised.

'But I thought you knew it was a brain tumour?' he asked as he handed me a tissue.

From this morning forward, something in me changed, or maybe I split in two. The hopeful me versus the fearful me. This diagnosis could never be a fixed state – I knew this, I think I always did, but I allowed myself to believe in spite of what I knew to be true. Although at least 70 per cent of the tumour could be removed, the remaining glioma, that 30 per cent, would always be inoperable and it could always mutate. I had faith in the unforeseeable, but the horror had embedded itself and would remain. As time passed, I would often joke amongst friends that the remaining 30 per cent of resected tumour was like a third person in our marriage, and sometimes making that mischievous Princess Diana head tilt

11

gave me a sense of control. At other times, this felt like a bit part that I played for a baffled audience. A desperate attempt to armour the translucent woman who smelled citrus groves in hospital corridors and drafted eulogies in her head as she waited for the bus.

Over the next six years, we lived with a shapeshifting tumour that, for months at a time, responded well to treatment, before viciously mutating in ways even pioneering doctors found difficult to predict. Over time, volatility became our normal and I weathered the unpredictability: that lurch, deep inside, every time I saw his body hit the floor with another grand mal seizure that signalled yet more tumour growth. Despite regular 999 calls, and midnight dashes to A&E, I found a pathway through each crisis with the help of my husband's sparkling wit and his gracious heart. I clung on to the contours of his optimism and imagination, as though it were a magical rescue harness. Until the tumour stopped responding to the radiotherapy, the chemotherapy, the experimental drug trialling. And, just like that, my harness snapped.

In the late summer of 2018, I sat by my husband's bedside at King's College Hospital and calmly repeated what his oncologist had told me hours earlier. His brain cancer had aggressively developed past the point of further treatment, surrendering him to a cruel, coarse reality – a place that science couldn't reach. He had been given weeks to live. Even now, my mind wanders back to the hospice room into which he was eventually moved. Me frantically fetching laundry each morning; him sitting heroically in his wheelchair, willing himself to resist, to survive, to live. He willed himself, fearlessly, for six excruciating weeks. He was only 41 years old.

In the weeks that followed my husband's death, I think there was a small part of me that expected nihility, obliteration, a big bang followed by nothingness. There was a presumption, inspired by all the art and literature that I had consumed over the years, that my heart would simply stop beating, that the shock would fell me before I had even ordered his cremation certificate and arranged the funeral service. It's the ultimate tragedy, isn't it? A love cut short. I am reluctant to mention the most famous star-crossed lovers, Romeo and Juliet, because they seem a far too obvious, dare I say clichéd, choice, but this was the first play I read at school, and it had an impact on how I viewed love and grief. Literature teaches us that there is romance in death. It gives us, the reader, a clear and unambiguous ending. Juliet isn't the only female protagonist whose grief and trauma lead her to an extreme self-sacrificing deed. Anna Karenina throws herself onto the railway tracks and into the path of a speeding train. Madame Bovary opens a jar of arsenic. Come to think of it, most of the literature I read in my impressionable teenage years was formed by the imaginations of men, and so my understanding of grief was shaped by them, too. An image of a woman on fire, a wheel of explosive powder sparking as she spins, so consumed by her losses, and by her luckless fate, that she burns herself out, quite spectacularly, in a brilliant blaze.

In reality, grief – much like life, and love, and death – is a far more nuanced and confusing state of play. It weighs you down and drags you around. Weeks stretch inside a shapeless void where the only certainties you're faced with every day are absence and existence. His and yours. Grief is neither a romantic, opium-fuelled Coleridge poem, nor a beautiful and stylised Millais painting. It is messy and rough; it is unforgiving and cruel. An encompassing pressure that made my head feel pushed and squeezed, compressing my everyday thoughts as though I were permanently clamped in a vice.

If you were to ask me what acute loss feels like, I'd motion you to the pub toilet in which I tasted my husband's ashes, ten minutes after I'd ordered a club sandwich for lunch with an empty casket lodged between my feet. If grief resides anywhere, it's here – a juncture where memories pinball the walls and a surreal delirium takes over the brain, yet somehow life around you carries on. Minutes after I watched the grains of my former life disappear down the plughole, I wiped the dust from my cheeks, shook down both dungaree legs, pulled up my socks, and rejoined my mum and best friend at the lunch table outside. The deed had been done, leaving a smoky oesophageal trail that permeated my body, leaching out through my pores. I swished it down with gulps of ginger beer and reached for another bite of my sandwich, telling neither of my fellow diners what I had just done.

I first felt this stealthy derangement 24 hours after I received The Call in the early hours of the morning – the call that told me my husband had died in his hospice bed whilst I slept restlessly at home. On a drab Saturday morning I sat silently in a third-floor visitor room, a few feet away from where he had taken his final breaths, and absently scanned the bookshelf in front of me. Row upon row of novels that might be flicked through in a traumatised daze, but never really read in the way that books should. Like the tepid mug of tea that was brought to me as I waited to collect my husband's belongings, everything here seemed unexceptionally normal and therefore obscenely wrong. *An innocuous room filled with unremarkable things*, I thought. A desperate place where hope dwindles between the shelves.

When I finally brought it all home – his rucksack, a death certificate and three plastic carrier bags filled with his possessions – I lined it up in our kitchen like groceries left to unpack. Opening and emptying, I grouped his things in neat categories on the floor, methodically logging every item like some kind of grief administrator. *The mundanity of everyday life*, I thought to myself as I surveyed the flotsam. *An extraordinary man reduced to these piles of ordinary things*. Unopened packets of biscuits, bags of crisps, a half-used bottle of shower gel, a box of uneaten chocolates. Jogging bottoms, sweaty t-shirts, a couple of battered magazines. Marcel Proust's *In Search of Lost Time*. A laptop. One iPad. His notepads – one, two, three, four of them – the ones he stacked in a Jenga-style tower next to his pillow whilst he slept.

He was halfway through writing a memoir exploring memory and consciousness when his brain tumour advanced and, like so many hospital inpatients, his nursing bed quickly became his world. A tiny nook where he could reclaim some semblance of normalcy, order and control. As a day-visiting wife, I quickly learned not to rearrange his belongings, realising that each item signified something in this borderland between life and death. Crammed into hospice carrier bags, that meaning now seemed permanently lost, but I still grasped at them anyway: a tired, listless attempt to recover any remnants that I could. I carefully fished out his headphones, wrapped the cable in neat loops around the headband, and placed them inside his office desk drawer. There was an upsetting correlation between the unopened packet of biscuits and the notepad that trailed off into nothingness on page five, and as I excavated more and more, the act of retrieval, this perverted lucky dip, led me to his dressing gown at the bottom of the plastic. I placed my head between the handles, shut my eyes, and closed the bag tightly around me, breathing him in, breathing him out, whilst crude memories span and whirled.

The smell brought me back to those first days in the summer of 2018, on a bustling ward at King's College Hospital, waiting for news from his oncologist five miles away at UCH Macmillan Cancer Centre. After years of drawn-out tests and treatments, what-ifs and maybes, his deterioration and subsequent hospital admission happened at breakneck speed, within a matter of days. One moment he was complaining of a tremor, and the next I was cutting up his sausage and mash into bite-size chunks, aeroplaning him mouthfuls of food, wondering at what point I should dial 999 to ask for help. *What constitutes an emergency?* I thought to myself. *What makes a tragedy? Had it already occurred last week when I heard a thump and a yelp from our bedroom and rushed down, two steps at a time, to find him splayed on the floor? Was it here in our kitchen, right now? Had I already witnessed it unfold in front of me, watching him turn on the taps and absent-mindedly saunter away from the washing up, leaving the water dangerously close to overflowing onto the floor?*

I made the call that evening and waited for the flashing blue lights to twinkle outside, a silent alarm on a Friday night that was watched by a sloshed queue of revellers in the fish and chip shop over the road. The doctors in A&E couldn't be 100 per cent certain, but it was probable that his uncontrollable tremors and facial drooping indicated disease progression, which would explain the minor stroke that had probably occurred days, maybe weeks, before.

After years of steady uncertainty, the pedal was pushed, the throttle valve opened. At the point where we began discussing hospice waiting lists, I sat cross-legged on a sweaty mattress staring blankly at a blood pressure monitor trolley whilst my husband meticulously took me through all the things I would need to know when the time came. Building society log-ins, email passwords, insurance numbers, updated funeral wishes. A list of people – colleagues from work, friends from university, ex-girlfriends, distant relatives – who I would need to update each day with snippets of his worsening condition, highly edited, so as not to incite panic.

Despite his tremors, he still managed to grip his biro and shakily write down a list. I babbled about the book I was currently reading, loosely parroting highlighted sections of prose in order to drown out the gentle moans of the elderly patient next door. In times of struggle, these were the roles we steadfastly assumed for ourselves. Whereas I retreated into my subliminal self, he reached out into the world for facts and information as a way to control the things that frightened him. But now, on the edge of the precipice, this dualism between his realism and my imagination seemed at odds with what was happening.

'You know, this might just be our stickiest spot yet,' he said with a wide-eyed hopefulness I had come to depend on. But his instructive handover told me something different, something new. Fighting the urge to rip up the paper that nestled in his lap, I sat on my hands until I could feel the burning in my fingers turn into a creeping numbness over my knuckles, upwards and outwards, from hand to elbow, from elbow to shoulder, from shoulder to heart. When he was finally done, I folded the pages once, then twice, before sliding them into my handbag with a smile and a nod. Then I curled myself around him, deadened arms brought back to life, clinging to the parts of him that were still there.

We're warned of the dangers around us as soon as we can crawl to them. The speeding traffic on a busy road. The touch of an electrical appliance with wet hands. A sharp knife left dangling precariously on a kitchen work surface. My nine-year-old mother left her hometown of Gdańsk, a city on the Baltic coast of northern Poland, in the late 1950s, and if you were to ask her what Polish she can remember now, as a 72-year-old émigré, she would reel off a basic list of anxious parental commands: 'nie dotykaj!', *don't touch*; 'zatrzymaj!', *stop*; 'słuchaj!', *listen*. Childhood instructions that are etched onto her brain but have little relevance to the present day, to the life she's in or the language she now speaks. In the days after my husband's death, I read and re-read his hospital handover notes with a similar kind of displacement. He had compiled this protective guidebook with a tenderness that belied the aggressive speed at which his tumour cells were reproducing and dividing, and now it was up to me to action them.

Only, what use was this practical manual, giving me shared access to a digital existence, when I couldn't even figure out where he was, corporeally and spiritually? The pension passwords and bank account sort codes I had been left with seemed as foreign to me as my mother's pidgin-Polish. My husband may as well have been standing in the middle of our living room, waving his arms and yelling 'słuchaj!' for all the help this notepad was giving me. Which is probably why I found myself hurtling towards Foyles bookshop in the West End of London on a weekday afternoon, with a crumpled list of authors in my handbag and my unwashed hair scrunched into a bun. When all rationality seeped away from my life and I began to contract, an inner voice intercepted and told me what I needed to do, where I needed to go, in order to defibrillate my heart: a quest that felt urgent. A dose of electric current to shock me back into life.

'Do not think that grief is pure, solemn, austere and "elevated" – this is not Mozart's *Requiem Mass*,' American novelist Joyce Carol Oates writes, unflinchingly, in her 2011 memoir, *A Widow's Story*. 'Think of crude coarse gravel that hurts to walk on. Think of splotched mirrors in public lavatories. Think of towel dispensers when they have broken and there is nothing to wipe your hands on except already-used badly spoiled towels.' Like a thirsty nomad, I lapped up Oates' writing in the immediate weeks that followed my husband's death. Joan Didion's work quickly followed, as I instinctively turned to memoirs about grief to help me make sense of the leaden butterflies that lurched and jerked deep inside me. The anguish that burned through my limbs, day after day. The night terrors, the back pain and the gravitational force dragging me slowly, slowly, down.

Although any compulsion is hard to rationalise, many readers of my journalism have enquired about my urgent need to read as a way to process my trauma. In all honesty, I hadn't considered my frenzied reading to be an unconventional act, or even a particularly unusual one. I've always been a voracious reader, but with time to reflect, I can now appreciate that this isn't the whole story and that there was more to my reading than simply an appetite for books. I recently discovered that the hottest stars in our night sky appear to us as a blue light, not red, yellow, or even white. When a new star is born, its fiery core is formed as it collapses under its own weight, its gravitational force pulling its gases to the centre, where it heats up, condenses, and starts to glow.

It started with a single book. When I passed through the automatic doors of Foyles, I made a beeline for a copy of Rainer Maria Rilke's collection of letters entitled *The Dark Interval* and began to read an excerpt italicised on the inside flap of the dust jacket:

'Where things become truly difficult and unbearable, we find ourselves in a place already very close to its transformation.'

Something in my core began to jostle and glow, and the tips of my ears grew hotter. I returned the book to its shelf. A minute later, I picked it up again. Flicking through the pages, I skimmed over words that seemed to gleam and flicker like glowing kernels as my eyes darted back and forth. I purchased the book and brought it home. Sat cross-legged against my radiator, I read condolence letter after condolence letter, each one written by the poet to grieving acquaintances or friends – from concert singers to astronomers to art collectors and even ex-lovers – most of them written in the immediate days after a loved one's death. Over the course of his life, Rilke wrote approximately 14,000 letters and here were just a few of them. I lingered on a fragment written on 9 October 1915, a letter Rilke sent to a woman called Ilse Erdmann who was struggling with the death of her nephew. In it, he wrote of the here and now, of our relationship with the earth, and he referenced the seeds of particular flowers that had journeyed here as stardust trapped inside the flaming rock of a meteorite. I read on. Yes, he wrote, it is possible 'to have the starred skies closely wrapped around one's heart'.

At the same time that I was devouring lyrical condolences from an eccentric poet, letters from my own friends and family began to drop on my doormat, day after day. Greetings cards adorned with consoling images of sunflowers and flocking starlings and a full moon over transient cherry blossom. *Thinking Of You*, one read. *Deepest Sympathy*, said another. I grazed on some, I left others unopened, stacking them in a neat pile in the spare room of our basement, far away from our living room bookshelves where I would reach for spines each night, imbibing words written by strangers because the deeply personal writing of those I knew was simply too much for me to process. Too much love, too much sadness, too much concern. Each letter seemed to stifle the air with emotions I didn't know how to express for myself.

I was lonely, yes. But I wasn't alone. The books I read enabled me to both disconnect from the world around me and engage with the microcosm inside. They provided me with companionship, they gave me fuel. I felt like Prospero in Shakespeare's mystical play *The Tempest*, a shipwrecked sorcerer whose magical powers are found between the pages of his books. It is said that the character of Prospero was inspired by an earlier anonymously authored play entitled *The Rare Triumphs of Love and Fortune*, which features an exiled magician Bomelio who lives in a cave with his books. When his son burns them, he goes mad because without them his spirit is lost.

'He that hath lost his hope, and yet desires to live.'

Reading was the only way I could seize autonomy in a body that scared me and in a world that looked scorched and strange. That was where the magic was. That was where I discovered my own wizardly power. It wasn't a mindful exercise to distract me from what was happening in my life. I wasn't looking to be pulled away from the pain I was feeling. Quite the opposite, in fact. I wanted to engage with it, I needed to understand. With time to consider, I'm sure that my analytical approach was heavily influenced by my many years as a journalist, jotting down questions and pointing my Dictaphone at all the things that both intrigued and baffled me. It wasn't long after I bought my copy of Rilke's letters that I began frequenting the Wellcome Library, perusing topics as wide-ranging as animal mourning, dream consciousness and theoretical physics. I was looking for context. I read, first and foremost, to understand, and I was only able to do this by exploring the words of others: scientists on a mission to crack the meaning of time, psychologists pursuing theories on the complicated mechanisms of bereavement, as well as literary writers who reflected my own distortions, approaching their grief with a similar voyeurism.

A colleague of mine had recommended Joyce Carol Oates' memoir. Plunging into her prose, I instantly recalled the first days I had spent sifting through my husband's everyday belongings, anaesthetised by the simultaneous sanctity and banality of such a task. It would take me months to process it all. His depleted deodorant. The ball of knotted laptop power cables. The iPhone I would have to momentarily switch on in order to permanently disconnect.

This isn't to say there is a one-size-fits-all narrative that can perfectly match anyone's grief. No loss is ever that straightforward. But I do think there is a universality to trauma that can break down the wall between two experiences, however divergent they may initially seem. Whether a death is sudden and unexpected, or prolonged and anticipated, it has the power to colonise any griever with the same frightening brutality. When Oates' husband of 47 years, Raymond Smith, died of a secondary infection after contracting pneumonia, disbelief quickly morphed into derangement and she quickly became a daily bereavement diarist, chronicling her erratic behaviour with brutal honesty. It's an account many grievers will recognise, but few would ever consider logging in its minutiae and actually publishing. Which is what attracted me to Oates' writing in the first instance: she doesn't shy away from the truth, nor does she sugar-coat it for her readers, either. And so, when I came face to face with the reality of my own widowhood, her stories reeled me in. Two thirds of the way through her 400-page journal we find Oates on her hands and knees at 4am, sobbing as she gropes for a misplaced sleeping pill that has rolled behind the toilet in her bathroom. It might just be one missing capsule, but without any meaning to guide her, she writes, her intimate world has been reduced to an overwhelming wasteland of *things*.

It's a narrative that is repeated by the doyenne of reportage, Joan Didion, in her grief memoir *The Year of Magical Thinking*. When her husband, the writer John Gregory Dunne, collapsed from a fatal heart attack on the living room floor of their Manhattan apartment in 2003, her rejection of reality led to a period of *'magical thinking'* in a world where realism came up short, a renunciation which also brought her to a world of things. T-shirts, sweatshirts, socks. Yes, Didion publicly acknowledged his death – she stacked up his clothes and gathered up the bags – but, inwardly, there were doubts. Or maybe there was hope. Either way, she couldn't give away the rest of his shoes. There was a magic trick still waiting to be performed, an inner voice interjected and, in the absence of rationality, she listened. How could she give away her husband's shoes, it asked. He would need his trainers when he finally returned home.

It may seem irrational, but when the life you recognise dissolves overnight, random, mundane objects – an unopened packet of biscuits, a bottle of sleeping pills or a battered pair of running shoes – suddenly take on new meaning. When the unthinkable happens, the impossible becomes imaginable. I didn't tidy away my husband's half-used bottle of shower gel because I genuinely believed he would knock on the front door one day like some kind of twenty-first-century Lazarus demanding to know where it was. I returned it to the shelf because that's where he had always reached for it. That's where it belonged. Remove a widow's sense of order and control and there isn't an awful lot to guide her in this completely alien world other than random artefacts and memories. Which is why this emphasis on *things* strikes me as a logical component of any bereavement process. In the vast hinterland of loss, they act as strange totems precisely because they are the only tactile scraps that have been left behind. It's what dragged a critically acclaimed novelist onto her hands and knees at 4am. It's what persuaded a Pulitzer Prize-nominated journalist that her husband might return and need shoes to walk in. And it's what convinced me to hold on to a used can of shaving cream instead of tossing it into the bin.

It is pointless to battle the thrust and drag of grief, just as it is futile to question the strange things it can make you do. Overpowered by the weight of my own cumbersome body, I would regularly sprawl out on the living room floor with my bundle of books. The coolness of the birch wood laminate gave me something else to feel against the taut surface of my skin. In this newly transformed, companionless space, crammed full of our trinkets and things, language darted around me as I hurtled from page to page. Urgent words. Visceral words. Verbs like *obliterate* and *mangle*. Adjectives like *bruised* and *desiccated*. Nouns like *stump* and *pain*. As days morphed into weeks and weeks morphed into months, reading became an act of intimate, anatomical exploration. I peeled back my skin and probed at the threadlike sinews underneath. Stripped back, cut asunder, I traced over the connective tissues that bound me together with a radically altered, penetrative gaze.

For weeks after my husband's death, I fixated on his battered toothbrush, wrestling with the senselessness of it all: the banality of everyday belongings, yet the holy significance of them, too. The way that time can shrink and stretch. After six protracted years governed by a chronic illness that defied predictability, my husband's deterioration would last no longer than six weeks. Forty-two days. 1,008 hours. A sudden rocking in our rowboat as the water seeped in over the sides and I frantically scooped out what I could, battling against the flow. It was an act of sheer defiance and I sustained it until the end, but where did this leave me now? In a blazing world of arbitrary things. Sat on the edge of our bath clutching my husband's toothbrush as if it was some kind of magical wand that might restore a missing part of him.

Similarly to Didion and her husband's shoes, I held on to it for longer than any rational person might expect. Over the last six years, I had fed myself stories in order to escape the reality around me – and here was another.

I never believed that our rowboat would submerge.

TWO

Shooting stars aren't really stars at all. And they don't exactly *shoot* so much as fall through the earth's atmosphere as a flaming ball of metallic rock that can blaze from orange to violet to red as it hurtles towards us. Astronomers can forecast a meteor shower, delicate streams of celestial debris that streak the opaque sky like fine silver rain, but random meteors are harder to predict. In 2018, a 50-kilogram fireball was witnessed by the residents of Hamburg, Michigan as an explosive flash of bright white light against the evening sky – a blinding flare that also caused an atmospheric shock wave equivalent to a 2.0-magnitude earthquake. Pebble-sized fragments of this inter-stellar fireball were later discovered on the frozen surface of two nearby lakes, the icy water preserving the shards of meteorite like freshly plucked marigold petals.

As a child, restless in bed, I would often pinch the corners of my closed eyelids in order to create glittering trails, cosmic explosions of colour, that would hypnotise me into sleep as I followed their lines and curves. I encountered insomnia and night terrors from a young age although, even now, I'm unsure as to what really caused them. The darkness seemed to bring out all my fears in the same way that the night sky perfectly backdrops burning cosmic ore. I could never make out its form – the Goliath-sized monster that chased me in my dreams – but

I always felt the quickening dilation of time as I tried to run away from it. The *thump-thump-thump* of my heart as I fled my imagined ogre. The shake and tremor as my hot, clammy heels pounded the ground.

My recurring childhood nightmare, like all nightmares, may have seemed like a never-ending torment, but I always woke with a sudden jolt in the dark. It was this tug of reality that convinced me I could be my own hero. A physical jerk that pulled me out of myself and led me to believe that it's entirely possible to save yourself from the frightful monsters in your mind. In the immediate months after my husband's death, reality and delusion overlapped so seamlessly that this belief lost all credibility. There can be no sudden jolt when the monster is made real.

I often wandered through our flat in the early hours of the morning mistaking shadows for ghosts in a hypnotised state: a semi-death to which I wilfully relinquished myself in order to stay close to him. In this altered universe anything was possible. An abandoned vacuum cleaner on the floor transforms into a nestling torso. A potted house plant grows into a towering oak tree. During daylight hours, I wore his white and navy letterman cardigan and brushed its cuffs against my skin in an attempt to replicate his soothing strokes, a subconscious habit I employed as I went about my day, bagging up his socks and underwear. His footprints trailed all over the house and it was futile to try to ignore them. I tackled his desk drawer of music badges on a random weekday night listening to The Kinks. An airline ticket stub flew out from his tatty paperback copy of Thomas Pynchon's *Gravity's Rainbow* (make of that what you will) as I was flicking through its pages. I tripped over his childhood collection of Asterix comics whilst vacuuming the spare room. I found his credit card during a routine search for my Converse trainers, and with a reverence one might pay a priceless holy relic, stroked my thumb over the braille numbering of the expiry date – *11/20* – before placing it back inside his wallet.

Laminated plastic still waiting to be swiped. An old boarding pass with no anecdote to account for it. Beloved objects, priceless memorabilia, with stories left to tell.

I immersed myself in his things, in his stuff, and then I took them to bed with me. Hours later I woke up drenched in sweat, caught in the act of trancelike retrieval. A tabletop widow with a search warrant, pawing at the mattress, clambering over pillowcases, looking for him between the sheets. It would take me 30 seconds after I woke from dreaming for my brain to catch up with my body. For my mind to inform it, like a frightened child in the dark, that my husband wasn't under the bedcovers. He'd gone, passed somewhere beyond me. Somewhere unfathomable, unreachable. *But, where?* a tiny voice asked me, desperate for answers. *But where?*

I could use words such as *disorientation* or *confusion* in order to describe this particular period in my early grief but, if I'm truly honest, neither of these seems up to the task. I'm not sure that the right word even exists. I'd argue that we need to create a new adjective to truly convey the turbulence that follows the severing of a heart. How can I possibly relate the feeling of total absenteeism? I was physically in the room and yet I was millions of light years away from everything that surrounded me and everyone I conversed with. It was only when I climbed into bed and switched off the light that the constraints of everyday life were loosened and I was able to fully immerse myself in my grief. It whirled around me – not a dream or a nightmare but a space between worlds where my body and brain could ignite and misfire, trying to make sense of something that was beyond all comprehension.

Whilst my nights were spent sleepwalking through the shock, my days were dedicated to concealing this confusion, albeit unconsciously. I would chatter away with the barista in my local cafe, skimming through the usual topics – the weather, the latest Brexit headlines, the book she was currently reading – before sitting at a table, stirring sugar into my coffee, battling the sounds that reverberated around the room and into my ears. The vibrations of a world continuing to spin felt like an assault. And yet I was powerless to stop the elderly woman from chattering, the coffee machine from grinding, the dog from barking, the cash register from pinging.

Perhaps it was because I felt so powerless that I internalised my day-to-day distress. It boomeranged and resurfaced in other ways, prickling and stinging like wildfire over my skin, starting with a gentle hum but swiftly intensifying into a kind of guerrilla warfare – clusters of contradicting symptoms that ambushed me as I attempted to fill out death registration forms and funeral paperwork. Fasciculations, muscle weakness, tingling and throbbing aches. One morning I swivelled out of bed only to find that I couldn't feel my left foot. I limped around the house for the rest of the day, stretching and levering my leg in order to awaken my toes. In the early evenings, numbness yielded to agitation. My hands and feet mutated into burning paddles that throbbed and pulsed as I sat on the sofa watching mindless comedies on a flickering screen.

My body was malfunctioning, and yet for all its rogue tactics, I still managed to create some semblance of a structured life. I got up every morning and showered and dressed. I drank coffee amongst strangers. I frequented solicitors' offices and funeral parlours. I filled out legal forms and documents. I vacuumed and ironed. I went out for dinner with friends.

If you were to have asked me the year before, I would have deemed all of these activities unthinkable so soon after my husband's death, and yet when the time finally came, it was these necessities of everyday living that kept me on my feet. We might want to believe in the romance of oblivion but when reality hits it just isn't doable. Life intervenes. The world still demands our participation. At a time when I wished to dissolve and disappear, I put on my reading glasses and set to work, filling out paperwork at my kitchen table – not because I wanted to but because I had obligations to fulfil, death duties to perform. At the same time that I was magicking Ikea house plants into skyscraping wishing trees I was also ringing utility companies, cancelling mobile phone contracts and ordering Marks and Spencer sandwich platters for the funeral buffet. On a lacklustre Monday afternoon, four days after his death, my parents drove me to Bromley Civic Centre to register it: entry 289.

Cause of death: *I (a) Glioblastoma*
Name and surname of informant: *Katharine Anne LISTER*
Qualification: *Widow of deceased, in attendance*

I sat in a small, stuffy office and watched an equally small and stuffy registrar type out the particulars at her desk. I had been expecting to break down uncontrollably, and had even prepared myself for it in the car, but her keyboard tapping robbed the moment of any profundity and, if anything, I felt irritated by the whole procedure. Didn't he deserve better than this? A beige cubbyhole that smelled like musty carpet and stale breath? This wasn't what I had expected at all.

'How many copies would you like?' she asked, finally lowering her spectacles.

'How many do I need?' I heard myself laugh incredulously.

'Most people request around four or five.'

'Well then, I guess I'll take five.'

'We charge £4 per copy,' she replied.

A few minutes later I joined a queue at the reception desk with order number 107989 in one hand and my Visa debit card in the other. I tapped four digits into the handset and, after the £20 transaction was approved, I was handed an A4 wallet to which I added his passport, recently renewed, void of stamps.

Anger isn't always expressible in the moment. A week later, I was sitting in a dazed state in a brasserie restaurant in south-west London with my parents on their ruby wedding anniversary. The waiter hovered, I ordered the fishcakes. The day before I had strolled across to my neighbourhood florist and ordered a bouquet to be placed on a coffin that nobody would see. His family and I had decided that he wouldn't want us to witness the cremation itself despite the instructions he had written years previously. In his final weeks, bedside conversations altered his typed instructions and he scribbled down a new set of directions which I kept in our kitchen dresser drawer. As with most junctures in life, things change, circumstances alter, wishes evolve and revise. Nonetheless I wanted to bring him something, physically carry it, a love token cradled in my arms, walked from my door to his. The florist suggested rosemary for remembrance and forget-me-nots for everlasting love, a detail I now replayed as my fork cleaved open my salmon lunch, cutting mouthfuls of poached egg amid the clutter and the din of lunchtime service. All whilst fighting the urge to scream.

George Bonanno, a professor of clinical psychology at Columbia University who has conducted more than two decades of scientific studies on grief and trauma, coined the phrase 'coping ugly' to illustrate how grief can take multiple forms. I first encountered Bonanno on a trip to the Wellcome Library and was drawn to his methodical approach, equal parts empathic and analytical, an approachable blend of scholarship I respected and admired. Over the last 25 years, Bonanno's Loss, Trauma and Emotion Lab in New York City has centred its research around the question of human resilience, analysing how people cope with loss and trauma. Its investigations read like a pessimist's checklist – from terrorist attack to traumatic injury, to divorce, job loss, bereavement, global epidemic and even military combat – but their findings from crisis to crisis, however divergent, have been fairly universal. We are more resilient than we give ourselves credit for, Bonanno insists. Not only that, but there are multiple pathways we can take to help us cope with extreme events.

In order to explain the phrase 'coping ugly' – a motto I parroted as my own in the winter of my grief – Bonanno uses the example of a football stadium that's been converted into an emergency shelter during Hurricane Katrina. You're trapped, he theorises, the conditions are unfamiliar, and you might behave erratically as a result, but this adaptive response is a key survival tactic in an uncertain world. It's one of the few bereavement terms I can actually identify with when I recall those first few days dangling in the abyss; my sweaty hands palmed on our cool bathroom tiles – just like Oates, searching for her lost sleeping pill – as I retched and spluttered on my knees. An hour later, I was back to flicking through funeral brochures, weighing up the benefits of biodegradable willow caskets and eco-friendly bamboo urns.

Grief patterns don't follow a blueprint, despite what we've traditionally been told. About a week after my husband's funeral, I found myself in the bowels of the British Library, flicking through a paperback book, *On Grief and Grieving: Finding the Meaning of Grief Through the Five Stages of Loss*, skimming over chapter headings like 'TEARS' and 'ANGELS' and 'DREAMS'. In 1969, Elisabeth Kübler-Ross, a Swiss-American psychiatrist, identified a range of emotional states experienced by terminally ill patients in response to their diagnosis, a theory that was swiftly re-interpreted and adapted by other practitioners to include those who grieve after a loved one's death. Denial, anger, bargaining, depression, acceptance. Since the 1970s onwards, these five stages, popularly dubbed the 'Kübler-Ross model', have come to define our understanding of loss, grief and mourning with little room for complexity, individuality and nuance – an evolution that has more to do with our reading of Kübler-Ross' theory over the years and the ways in which we've interpreted her stages as chronologically fixed.

I fell into this trap too, which is probably why I gravitated instead towards the roving memoir writing of Didion and Oates, although I certainly tried to take Kübler-Ross' itinerary on board. I got out my notepad and pen, but an hour later I was still staring at a blank page wondering why I felt so anaesthetised by an activity that had recently given me such purpose and intent. Despite an author's note that reassured me, the reader, that 'there is no correct way or time to grieve', the contents page, whether intentionally or not, implied a conflicting narrative with its capitalised sections – and the contradiction jarred in me. Whatever floats your grief-boat, I thought to myself, but this wasn't making sense to me. I slammed the book shut and brushed my fingers over the ethereal feathers that adorned the cover before returning it to the librarian with a decisive push across the counter.

Kübler-Ross always insisted that her five-stage model had been misunderstood, that it wasn't intended to prescribe any particular order, but I do wonder whether this misconception helps explain its sustained influence over the decades. The 'Five Stages' model, interpreted by mourners in a chronological way, might oversimplify a complex experience, and place adverse pressure to neatly conform, but it can also give them a sense of order at a time of acute social isolation and confusion. Yes, the notion of stages is flawed, but this flowchart approach to loss is an enduring and popular narrative for a reason. Fifty years since they were first introduced, Kübler-Ross' stages are still one of the most widely recognised grief theories, frequently referenced and endlessly analysed. It became a cultural phenomenon, too. Take *The Simpsons*, for instance – in the second season of the long-running show, Kübler-Ross' five stages of grief are parodied when Homer eats poisoned sushi and is later informed he has 24 hours left to live. Despite its critics, the Kübler-Ross model isn't going anywhere.

Ruth Davis Konigsberg, in her book *The Truth About Grief: The Myth of Its Five Stages*, attributes the ubiquitous influence of Kübler-Ross' theory to the decade in which it was first introduced, an era that saw a burgeoning, secular self-help movement transform into a new creed, filling the void that was left behind by religious faith. I was reminded of Konigsberg's writing on a recent trip to Italy's Adriatic coast, wandering through the Basilica della Santa Casa – a pilgrimage shrine in the small hilltop town of Loreto – breathing in incense and marvelling at the lapis lazuli-hued domes that towered above me.

Legend has it that the enshrined House of the Virgin Mary was transported to the eastern coast of Italy by angels from Nazareth in 1294 and dropped into a patch of laurel trees, a story that still attracts thousands of believers who flock to it every year seeking transformation, guidance and salvation. As

I walked through the elaborately sculpted marble columns of the Santa Casa di Loreto I passed dozens of pilgrims kneeling under a golden statue of the Virgin, bowed in silent prayer, and felt slightly jealous as I did so, unmoved in my own scepticism but envious nonetheless of their faith. How much easier it would be, I whispered to my friend Jon, if I could believe in all of this. Adopt a story, light a candle, pick a pew – and belong somewhere. Subcontract someone else, or should I say some*thing* else, to tell me where to go, and how to grieve, and what to believe.

I spotted a clear Perspex box to the right of a flickering votive candle rack and felt its frame with my fingers. The instructions in English read:

> 'In this casket you can put all your requests, they will be
> exposed to the Madonna's view. Be sure she will listen
> to you because she is our mother.'

Curiosity got the better of me and, peering through the acrylic, I caught snippets of pleading lines on a folded square of paper, scrawls of biro from a father who had lost contact with his three sons. A desperate message in a bottle, propelled by hope, and who was to say that his hope was misguided? What made my quest for truth any more legitimate or credible? How could I possibly critique this jumble of tombola prayers when it was demonstrating something I was still looking for, so many months after my own separation? A release from the past. An opportunity to speak of my pain, and in turn, be held and heard.

I wonder if this explains why I didn't sidestep the Five Stages completely. No one is that Teflon. Although I struggled to identify with the neat transitions of the Kübler-Ross model, I still found myself looking to them for guidance from time to time in a similar fashion to the kneeling pilgrims I encountered in Loreto gazing up at their blessed Lady, full of grace.

Despite my renunciation of its structure, I regularly questioned why I wasn't processing my husband's death in a smoother way. On a midweek night in September 2018, I sat in my local cinema bar with Andy, sipping beer and discussing the guest list for my husband's impending funeral. During the course of our conversation my mind wandered from eulogies and memorial music to the Marvel film we were about to watch and the plot line of its predecessor which I hadn't seen and, despite my questioning that evening, had no real interest in understanding better. I even bought a box of popcorn. When we sat down in our seats I was suddenly reminded of the last time I had been in this screening room – with both my husband and Andy. We had been a few minutes into the opening credits of another sequel, this time for *Blade Runner*, when the cinema's fire alarm began to beep; we were evacuated into the lobby much to Andy's annoyance and my husband's amusement. The memory brought the blood to my cheeks, inflaming both sides of my face as I reached into the popcorn box and shovelled a handful of dry kernels into my mouth.

It would take time for me to realise that grief is anything but linear, that there are no stages to be ticked off, only motion sickness, as you career from one mood to the next, desperately trying to mimic some semblance of everyday life. As a consequence, my memory of this time is pretty sketchy and it isn't always something I can fully trust. My prose might seem assured, but the retrospection is flawed. Grievers aren't always the most reliable narrators. I can tell you that I went to the theatre a month after my husband died, but I cannot cite the play. I remember laughing hysterically in a pub, but I remember nothing of what was said. Perhaps impermanence is key here. If the process of grief isn't linear then it follows that subsequent memories aren't either. In the cosmic void of loss, you need to look a little closer at the pinwheel. Yes, it is possible to detect spiral galaxies in the night sky through a standard pair of binoculars, but it is only by examining long exposure photographs that you can truly appreciate the rotating halos of stars and dust that constitute its swirling form. The elliptical orbit of blood-red capillaries that whirl around its core.

Many writers before me have likened the disorientation of grief to being geographically lost, whirling and spinning as they try to locate themselves. In Deborah Levy's *The Cost of Living*, the British novelist describes the weeks after her mother died as a directionless period that felt to her 'as if some sort of internal navigation system was drifting'. In *A Grief Observed*, C.S. Lewis wrote of ever-repeating circles after the death of his wife, Joy Davidman:

'For in grief nothing "stays put". One keeps on emerging from a phase, but it always recurs. Round and round.'

Although she never formally wrote of her grief, I remember visiting the Brontë Parsonage Museum on a frosty November morning in 2016 and reading about Charlotte Brontë's evening laps around the dining room table after the deaths of her siblings, Emily and Anne – a frantic routine that was witnessed by Parsonage servant Martha Brown, and quoted in Elizabeth Gaskell's 1857 biography, *The Life of Charlotte Brontë*:

> 'For as long as I can remember – Tabby says since
> they were little bairns Miss Bronte & Miss Emily &
> Miss Anne used to put away their sewing after prayers,
> & walk all three one after the other round the table in
> the parlour till near eleven o'clock. Miss Emily walked
> as long as she could; & when she died Miss Anne &
> Miss Bronte took it up, – and now my heart aches to
> hear Miss Bronte walking, walking on alone.'

I reconstructed Charlotte Brontë's late-night circuits every morning that I circumnavigated the outer perimeter of our local park, looping round and round the recognisable wrought-iron lattices of Crystal Palace transmitting station, a towering 719-foot landmark that dominated my husband's hospice vista from the other side of the duck pond. I walked a great deal in the winter after his death, but the route was always the same, a voluntary tethering that kept me closely tied to the nerve centre, the HQ of my grief, the anchorage where he died. In his final days I would often stand at my husband's hospice window looking out onto the towering transmitter – affectionately nicknamed 'South London's Eiffel Tower' due to its correlative shape – and recall our many trips to the French capital, ambling through the cobbled streets of Montmartre, stopping for a seductive pastry or two. How far from Paris we were. How far from Paris I was now. When my mind stalled, my legs paced, and my thoughts would wander again. Movement begets movement. The park's wide, curved walkways gave me a recognisable path to follow when my brain wires tangled in an unruly knot of *how* and *why* and *what*, an altered state of consciousness I can best illustrate by enlisting the help of a nineteenth-century nonsense rhymer from Cheshire.

'What do you call yourself?' an inquisitive fawn asks Alice in *Through the Looking Glass*. 'I wish I knew!' she replies. When Lewis Carroll's adventurous hero steps through the mirror, she arrives at the wood 'where things have no names', and wandering under the bower of trees, forgets all nouns, including her own name. I've read a lot of non-fiction grief texts over the last year yet, to my mind, none captures the intricate relationship between memory, language and disassociation as succinctly as this fictional exchange between a seven-year-old girl and a talking deer. It speaks of the internal dislocation, of being lost in such a profound sense that it alters not only the way you see the world, but the way the world sees you.

I first became aware of this profound dissociation when looking at a photograph. It was taken three days after my husband's death, at an open-air Bavarian restaurant in Richmond. The sky is as pale as alabaster, the curvaceous body of the river is obscured, but the jade green tendrils of a weeping willow give the riverside

41

scene a pleasant backdrop nonetheless. There are pints of beer, and towering platters of bratwurst and mash. Two of my friends are sitting opposite me: one is taking the photograph, the other is eyeing up the feast. My father is there, too. I am smiling, we're all smiling, but look closer and my eyes aren't looking at the camera so much as looking through it, fixating on a faraway point. If every picture tells a story, this one is a tale of absence, of imperceptible orbits of dust. This is the story it *should* be telling us. In reality, my absenteeism is almost impossible to detect. This photograph cannot possibly relate the trauma I felt and internalised that day, as I followed the river's flow with my eyes, swallowing bites of Bavarian sausage as if they were red-hot coals.

Every time I look at my glazed expression, and the smiles all around me, I am reminded of the American essayist Susan Sontag's theory that all photographs are a kind of memento mori, a slicing and freezing of time – a tenet shared by Algerian-born French philosopher, Jacques Derrida. So much so, that he rejected his own image altogether. In a 2002 interview snippet posted on YouTube, a camera lens clunkily zooms in on raised eyebrows and flared nostrils as Derrida explains why he forbade the publication of any photographs of himself until 1979. He didn't want his experience to be framed, he answers the interviewer with a cautious pause, but his problem, he continues, wasn't simply theoretical – it was a mixture of narcissistic horror, of seeing his own face, as well as a kind of photographic thanatophobia. 'I don't like the death effect, so to speak,' he pushes on further into the void. 'The kind of death that's always implied when one takes a picture.'

If I had stumbled across this interview at any point before widowhood, I might have scoffed at this kind of statement, but when I look at the photograph in front of me, and my hand nervously gripping my father's left arm, I see its relevance. The static nature of the image feels at odds with my memory of that day, as fragmented as it is, of venturing out into the world and simulating a Sunday lunch at my husband's favourite eatery in order to affirm that I still existed in some way, that my surroundings could still hold me without him. Although this photograph documents that fraught moment, to some extent, it also deceives the observer, as all images inevitably do. Because when we seek to capture any moment in a single frame, we are, whether consciously or not, anticipating its demise. Time passes, context wanes, images fade, loved ones disperse. To a random observer, our trio of smiles indicates a carefree afternoon and nothing more. But to the widow returning to it a year after it was taken, this photograph is a brutal reminder of a fractured time she'd rather forget – and in many ways, already has. When I look at this image, I see comets, I see stars. I see a transparent woman trying to hold on to what is left, and what has gone.

Every photograph and every fable, even Alice's adventures in Wonderland, tells us something about loss. Perhaps that's why we hold on to them so tightly. Her zigzagging approach to chaos is something I also adopted in my first few months of grief, darting between avoidance and engagement. One morning, I finished my cup of coffee only to vomit it back up again before I had even had time to reap its caffeinated benefits. I'm not sure I even gave it much thought when it happened. I

43

simply pulled myself up, gargled some mouthwash at the sink, and returned to the kitchen where a binder of funeral brochures were waiting for me.

Not long after I rejected the five stages of grief, I read about another theory, only this one seemed to correlate with what was happening to me in a way that Kübler-Ross' couldn't quite manage, the way I kept veering from dispassionate pragmatism to violent distress. In the mid-90s, Margaret Stroebe and Henk Schut came up with a new way of approaching bereavement, calling it the Dual Process Model – a fairly uninspiring title for an enlightened concept that challenged the way we talk about loss. In it, they identified two responses after the death of a loved one, 'loss-oriented' and 'restoration-oriented', with mourners oscillating between both modes as they try to absorb what has happened. Grief, they proffered, isn't a structured or systematic process but a jumble of confusing emotions that can pinball you from wails to laughter to crippling self-doubt in a single day, sometimes in a single hour. This kind of seesawing might feel irrational, it might seem like you're losing grip on reality, but it is, in fact, a natural fluctuation. Yes, confrontation – recognisable emotions such as sadness and anger – plays a huge part, they argued, but respite from such painful emotions is equally integral.

Loss is a complex beast, and it doesn't always follow a single narrative strand. As Bonanno writes in his grief text, *The Other Side of Sadness*:

'Relentless grief would be overwhelming. Grief is tolerable, actually, only because it comes and goes in a

kind of oscillation. We move back and forth emotion-
ally. We focus on the pain of the loss, its implications, its
meanings, and then our minds swing back toward the
immediate world, other people, and what is going on
in the present. We temporarily lighten up and recon-
nect with those around us. Then we dive back down
to continue the process of mourning.'

I'll be honest, I was a little shocked to recall the plate of bratwurst and mash that I tucked into three days after my husband
died, but when I think about Stroebe and Schut's swinging
pendulum, it makes as much sense to me as my body's physical
need to howl and disgorge itself. Grief isn't a one-dimensional
experience, but an oscillating process that mirrors the natural
cycles we all learned about in biology class, the repeating patterns that can be found almost everywhere in our natural world.

Spirals, waves, tessellations, symmetry. Like the expanding
universe around us, we are a symphony of restless change. I
recently read that the outer layer of the sun's atmosphere, its
corona, is so hot that its charged particles billow out into space
as solar wind. Here on earth, cresting waves can travel for thousands of miles before they surrender themselves, effervescent
arches that roar and boom as they return, over and under, to
where they began.

Sometimes, when I returned to our empty house, I was so
overwhelmed by the blazing rings of fire that throbbed around
the arches of my feet that bathing them in tepid water seemed
to be the only plausible way to cool them down. Hours after

my bratwurst lunch, I turned on the taps and curled into the tub. When I dunked my ankles into the water, they stung as they made contact, ten flaming toes that seemed to heat up the molecules around them, throbbing and flaring as they did so. Dipping my head beneath the surface, I tapped my fingernails against the porcelain below.

Dit dah, dit dah. I typed like intermittent Morse code. *Dit dah, dit dah.* I communed with him gently under the waves.

THREE

There was another way I could temper the flames and that was by perusing my husband's words in whatever format he had left them. I scrolled through WhatsApp messages and cherry-picked witty asides and mundane observations, a transformative act that reshaped them into one-off haikus. Old birthday cards he had sent me over the years were memorised in a similar fashion to prayer cards. I typed his name into my Gmail inbox and scrolled through hurried subject lines ('On train to Peckham shd b there 7 x') and chatty emails ('Did you know that in the early 70s The Stooges rehearsed and recorded in a studio in Wimbledon?'). Even practical documents became treasured artefacts in their own right. When my husband wrote out his funeral wishes in 2015 – or should I say, typed and printed them – he did so with his usual comic flair:

'If you are reading this then it's pretty likely that I'm dead. So the first thing for me to ask is – are you sure? Please could you double check? I might just be asleep. I'm a pretty sound sleeper, everyone knows that. Assuming that I haven't died in a horrible accident where I was ripped apart by wolves and then eaten so that you can't actually find the body, I'd like to be cremated. Honor Oak Crematorium seems nice. Plus it's on the east London line. You know what people from north London are like about coming south of the river.'

If you had ever chatted with my husband, you will immediately recognise this gallows humour because it defined the man he was and the patient he eventually became. On a weekday afternoon on the Rugby ward at St Christopher's Hospice, a volunteer and therapy dog padded up to his bed and when the unsuspecting woman earnestly asked him whether he'd like to give Max a stroke, he instantly replied, 'No thanks, I've already had one of those,' a quip that was recited by many of his friends, and quoted by the obituary writer assigned to relay his life and work on page 54 of *The Times*, the paper he worked for as Head of News Development from 2010 up until his death.

When the social media tributes multiplied, not every depiction seemed true to the multifaceted person he was and, at times, the misquotations and exaggerations rankled me. I was alarmed by the ease with which remembrances morphed as they were shared and repeated, not least because when a person dies, memories are all we're really left with. Take the above therapy dog anecdote, for instance. An appendage to this popular story is that, despite the wisecracking, he actually *did* give Max a stroke, and expressed delight in doing so. But that's the nature of legacy, I suppose. The stories we tell are always subject to truncation and embellishment as we shape the narrative to fit the way we see things. History is perspective. We want to relay an impression in addition to the facts, and sometimes the former takes precedence over the latter. Or at least, that's how it seemed to me when I came face to face with a broadsheet pull quote that read: 'It was rumoured that Chris Martin asked him to join Coldplay.'

I thought about Chris Martin and Max the dog when I flipped over his satirical funeral wishes and read the final sign-off:

'Please don't be sad. I'm off to join the universe and I'm excited.'

His sister read out this line at his funeral and, to my mind, those thirteen words were the true mark of the husband I had lost, revealing a purity and romanticism beneath the quicksilver wit. Some days they comforted me, other days they goaded me into battle, clashing with who, or against what, I'm still unable to say. On a random October evening, I met a friend at a neighbourhood pub, all smiles and chit-chat, gulping down beer in a futile attempt to suppress the flickers of nausea creeping upwards from my stomach, through my chest, and finally into my throat. I didn't want it to win that evening – 'it' being the relentless wildfire of my grief – but it whipped around me anyway, prickling across my forehead, raging deep down inside my belly. 'I'm really sorry, Jon,' I interrupted my friend's flow, 'but I think I'm going to be sick.' Reunited with the remnants of my earlier dinner, and the faint whiff of pine-scented chloride, something in me turned as my stomach heaved, again and again, into the oval target below. I had spent the last six weeks in the foetal position; shoulders arched, hands splayed, eyes down. I had to break the pattern, somehow. Get up, get out, take off. 'He's gone off to join the universe,' I looked up at Jon as he hovered silently in the doorway. 'And I'm down here – throwing up in a toilet bowl.'

Up until this moment, I hadn't wanted to be anywhere else. I had spent a lot of time on the floor between the months of August and November: reading books, writing notes, bagging possessions. I was safe there, I felt held. Time seemed to slow down with my back pressed up against the wall. When grief's gravitational force pulled me down, quite literally, it gave me the space I needed to disengage from the frantic day-to-day of early widowhood: texting friends and family, and all the cold, hard practicalities of death and dying, the many tedious tasks you are obligated to carry out and complete when you can't even say your husband's name without bursting into violent, unruly tears.

Slow it down, my legs moaned, *slow it right down*. I often slumped and crumpled, and when I did, the beating hands of my wristwatch became fainter and fainter until I could swear it had stopped ticking completely. When you watch a lethargic tumour suddenly shapeshift into a merciless executioner your understanding of time distorts, too. When my husband was first diagnosed in 2012 it felt as if an intruder had broken into our house. Over the next six years, that intruder took up residence with us, and we learned to live with it somehow, but it was never fully okay. I was always subliminally aware of its presence, even during the calmer periods when the oligoastrocytoma remained dormant.

Eventually it will wake up, I thought. Not today, and probably not tomorrow, but maybe next week, perhaps next month, or even next year. We tend to class 'quick deaths' as an instantaneous event without warning – a car crash, for instance, or a heart attack – but when my husband's chemotherapy finally stopped working in 2018, his six-week decline felt just as obscene.

After years of a permanent, protracted illness – so permanent, in fact, that we didn't even call it an illness, we referred to it as a condition – I watched his body rapidly atrophy with a slow horror. Time reared, and bucked, and threw us up into the air. Suddenly we didn't have enough of it. Within the space of a fortnight I was now washing his clothes, and feeding him his lunch, washing his hair, and tying his shoes. Four months previously we were sitting at a red-and-white gingham covered table, in a trattoria in Rome, eating unctuous pappardelle. Now I was sitting in a hospice family room with my head in my hands, rocking gently back and forth as a health worker went through a shortlist of care homes for the under-65s.

I didn't trust time anymore. Like a band of elastic it had stretched and pulled then shortened and shrunk until I didn't know what to do with it. Any notion of time as a measurable unit dissolved. My husband could have died yesterday, or last month, or last year. A day felt like a month. The last eight weeks? An hour.

The Italian theoretical physicist Carlo Rovelli calls it 'a loss of unity', the way that time can slow down and speed up. I had never concerned myself with quantum physics before – a decision that was largely based on my inability to grasp abstruse theories, as opposed to any general disinterest in them – but when my days started to expand and contract I paid attention.

Rovelli uses water and rock to make his point. Time passes more slowly at sea level than it does in the mountains, he writes, a difference so imperceptible that it can only be measured with precision clocks that one can buy (for a tidy sum) on the internet. In 2010, researchers at the National Institute of Standards and Technology in Colorado measured this gravitational time dilation by comparing the ticking of two identical atomic clocks, raising one to a height of a metre above the other. As predicted by scientists, the higher clock ticked at a slightly faster rate than its lower counterpart.

When I read about these precise clocks, my desire to ground myself made a little more sense. Maybe it was a primal instinct, I thought. If the earth's gravity warps time and space in this way, it didn't seem out of the realms of possibility that I was unconsciously seeking a slower movement of time. Night after night I would cross my legs and open another book, resting it against the diamond of space between my thighs, and for a short time I was content to melt into the lacuna – until something pushed back.

On a Friday lunchtime in late October, exactly two months after I collected my husband's things from St Christopher's Hospice, I peeled myself off the bathroom floor, packed a bag and boarded a flight to Seville with my toilet bowl-issued instructions sloshing about in my brain:

Get up, get out, take off.

The wheels went up and I was away, en route to meet my Spain-based friend Cila in arrivals with one version of myself left flailing on the tarmac and another ascending upwards, flying through the milk-white clouds. My first few days in the Andalusian capital were a bewildering mix of blue skies, winding cobblestoned streets and tropical palms. I grazed on greasy plates of deep-fried croquettes and salty pork chicharrónes, washing them down with amber glasses of fino in bustling tapas joints that, contrary to the popular *Cheers* theme, didn't know my name. On a bright and golden morning, we walked arm in arm through the Moorish arches of the Royal Alcázar's Patio de las Doncellas, the Patio of the Maidens, marvelling at the interlacing diamonds of leaves chiselled into the geometric plasterwork above.

In the evenings, we sat in lively bars, loitering under clusters of hanging Iberian jamón, with his name splicing our conversation like raindrops echoing in an empty bucket. Every night followed a similar pattern when we returned to our rented apartment. I'd get into my pyjamas, slide between the sheets, and anxiously wait for a wine-induced slumber to envelop me, but the rescue never came. Tossing and turning, flashes of memories whizzed past me, slide after slide, a Kodak carousel of moving projections that flickered onto the ceiling, bringing him back to life. The way he danced on pub dance floors, his drainpipe legs twisting and turning – knees bent, right foot raised – in preparation for a 360 degree twirl that whirled his body round and round. The way he laughed, I mean *really* laughed, the unmistakable hyena squeal that was launched high into the stratosphere with a backwards jerk of his head and a clap of hands to punctuate its descent. The way he soothed me when I couldn't sleep, index and middle finger tracing over my left eyebrow with gentle strokes, back and forth, half-asleep but still present in the darkness somehow.

I had succeeded in relocating myself to the mountain ranges of Andalusia, but time had other ideas for me. It's true what they say. There are no quick fixes for a broken heart. It wasn't as simple as placing an atomic clock over my head and hoping for a slightly quicker tick of the hands to erase time, void at least part of my day, fast forward past the gruesome bits like a TV remote pointed at the screen. The seconds beat. The raw footage plays on. Hearts pump with a steady *lub-dub*, *lub-dub*, *lub-dub*. Life keeps moving, that's true, but not at a pace you can control. After three sleepless nights in Seville we hit the road towards Cádiz with Cila at the wheel and me curled up in the passenger seat beside her. We barely spoke as the tarmac twisted and curved ahead, my eyes gazing up and around at the craggy slopes and jagged peaks of the Sierra de Grazalema Natural Park with the lilting sound of Echo and the Bunnymen fluttering through the car speakers. The sun streamed through the windshield and its rays tingled my pores, dancing on the surface, rekindling my cheekbones. It brought me back, I felt its warmth.

The Guadalete River, named after the Arabic phrase meaning *River of Forgetfulness*, ribbons itself around the hilltop town of Arcos de la Frontera in a province of Cádiz that perches high above the rocky cliffs. A fairytale kingdom waiting in suspense. When we pulled up outside Cila's front door, I swung my legs onto the gravel and sauntered across a children's playground to take a look at the vista that was to be my home for the next week. Squinting across the sloping grassland, my eyes roamed over the hotchpotch of whitewashed houses and wild foliage that scattered towards the San Cristóbal mountain. It wasn't long after my husband's death that Cila suggested I visit her here. Drink wine, read books, she'd cook. I hadn't been expecting a rescue package but she sent one anyway, tucking her invite into a collection of poems by an American writer called Jack Gilbert, a mournful poet whose grief and metre echoed my own.

'Like a wooden ocean out of control.
A bleached heart. A cauldron of cooling melt.'

Over the coming days I went on slow afternoon walks through the whitewashed pueblos blancos, picking up my sluggish legs as I determinedly climbed the steep winding steps. Threading through the narrow maze of cobbled streets, I looped round its teetering sixteenth-century church, the Iglesia de San Pedro, surveying the landscape as I did so, the vast swathes of poplars and ash trees that wended their way down to the water below. I walked and walked but at night sleep still didn't come. Each night I lay in Cila's spare room with thoughts of him encircling me, a gauze-like state that blurred the lines between reality and imagination so convincingly that I questioned their very existence. In my prolonged sleeplessness, grief smoked me out and smudged my surroundings. As 11pm morphed into 2am, and 2am evaporated into a 4am panic, his unearthly presence seemed to swirl around me. Inside out, mapping his trails, I caressed the air for him, I thought I heard him speak. And whilst there was no discernible form to any of my delusions, that didn't make the concept of an earthly visitation any less believable to me. It didn't render the sensations I was feeling any less real.

The word 'hallucination' was first introduced into the English language by physician and author Thomas Browne in 1646, derived from the Latin 'alucinari' meaning *to wander in the mind.* But for anyone who's ever experienced one, the encounter is a little harder to describe. Oliver Sacks called the hallucinatory experience 'an essential part of the human condition' – a peculiar description but an accurate one when you consider its widespread prevalence in our lives.

In his 2012 book, *Hallucinations*, the British neurologist separated the phenomenon into fifteen chapters in order to explore its varying shapes and forms, from imagined smells to invented sounds and even phantom limbs. Over his 50-year career, Sacks encountered a wide range of hallucinating people – both in his medical practice and in his correspondence with enquiring readers. A lady in her nineties who saw horses drudging over soft, swirling snow. A patient referred to as Stephanie W. who, prior to her treatment for narcolepsy, regularly saw what she described as an 'angel' over a particular motorway exit. His friend Liz, who, following a devastating break-up, was on the verge of swallowing a handful of sleeping tablets with her whiskey when she heard a voice say, *No. You don't want to do that.*

My husband hallucinated, too. Strange auras that signalled to him that an epileptic seizure was about to take place. I once asked him to describe them to me and he replied that he could feel them physically, a jumbled scrapbook of forgotten memories fired from the back of his brain to the frontal lobe. They hurt, he said, the painful darts inside his head. In 2017 he wrote about the persistent déjà vu that characterised his epileptic condition.

'I was lounging under a tree in a packed east London park when I experienced a sudden feeling of vertigo, followed immediately by an overwhelming and intense sense of familiarity,' he wrote for the Wellcome Trust, describing an occurrence that had taken place a few months previously. 'The people around me vanished and I found myself lying on a tartan picnic blanket amid a field of high golden wheat. The memory was rich and detailed. I could hear the sway of the wheat ears as a gentle breeze brushed through them. I felt warm sunlight on the back of my neck and watched as birds wheeled and floated above me.'

He always said that after every seizure, it felt as if a tiny piece of him had been permanently snatched away. I never said it out loud, but I could always sense this postictal absence, the unbridgeable distance, and I quietly ached for his return in full knowledge of the facts. That I couldn't occupy that space with him. That he didn't wish for me to occupy that space with him, either. It was his, and his alone, and we were both aware of its markings. Lying restlessly in a guest bedroom in Spain, something shifted in that narrative. Maybe it was madness, maybe it was wishful thinking, but I could sense our worlds overlapping as my own phantoms wheeled and floated in the early hours of morning, as if death was opening a door. I finally understood what he meant, how they felt, those painful darts inside his head.

Almost all amputees experience some kind of sensation when a part of their body is removed, a phenomenon referred to as a 'phantom limb'. For many, around 63 per cent, these sensations are painful, and the causes are still not clear. One popular theory is that the itches, burns, throbs and cramps are caused by a cortical remapping, a rewiring of the sensory system in response to the amputation. But there is no confirmed hypothesis. At least, there is no definitive explanation that I've been able to find in my research for this book. The more I have read about phantom limb pain, the more I have realised how challenging it can be to rationalise the pain amputees feel, and to understand it completely. Even the word 'pain' itself is rooted in myth, also the name of the she-dragon, Poena, a demon spirit summoned from the underworld by the Greek god Apollo to terrorise the mortal Argives.

If grief is pain, and pain is a response to loss, then maybe hallucinations are a useful construct to fill that void. A way for the griever to extricate themselves on their own terms, in their own time, of their own free will. Or maybe they are the disorientated brain's way of recreating an absent person as it would an amputated arm, a haunted state that Sacks describes as 'a painful longing for reality to be otherwise'. It's a summation that, to my mind at least, seems pretty rational. It also makes me wonder how we veered so far away from our own subtleties. How did we reach a place where our intricate mental processing is so little understood – the rewiring, the remapping, the sifting through. For Sacks, the misconceptions have been entrenched in us socially and culturally from generation to generation:

'Many cultures regard hallucination, like dreams, as a special, privileged state of consciousness – one that is actively sought through spiritual practices, meditation, drugs, or solitude. But in Western culture, hallucinations are more often considered to portend madness or something dire happening to the brain – even though the vast majority of hallucinations have no such dark implications.'

Ghosts, apparitions, phantoms, spectres. The language of grief does nothing to advance our understanding of its psychological complexities, and in particular, the delusional thinking that can occur after a death. Which is strange considering its ubiquity. Reading Sacks' conclusions, I was reminded of the hallucinatory experiences I read about in the Wellcome Library in the early months of my grief, in particular a phenomenon of visual apparitions that was recorded amongst the widows of the Native American Hopi tribe in Arizona. More recently in 2015, researchers at the University of Milan found that hallucinations triggered by loss were 'strikingly high'. Their evidence suggested that post-bereavement hallucinatory experiences (PBHE) ranged from 30 per cent to 60 per cent amongst the widowed subjects they studied, 'giving consistence [*sic*] and legitimacy to these phenomena'.

Bereavement delusions aren't always easy to define, which can make them all the more alienating for the person encountering them. Before my husband died, I had considered hallucinations to be something visible or audible. A ghostly figure at the foot of your bed. Or a babbling voice where there is none. The reality, for me, was far more oblique than this. To this day, I've never seen a resurrected manifestation of my husband, despite wishing for it sometimes, but over the last eighteen months I have experienced hallucinatory sleep disturbances that have obliterated my sense of self – quite literally.

The first of these occurred in the days that preceded his funeral, a sudden jolt in the dark followed by what I can only describe as amnestic panic; a total evaporation of memory; the inability to recall who I am, or where I am, or what this is, what any of this is: the shelf to the right of me, that dressing table in the corner of the room, this bed that I'm lying on. As time has moved on, the night delirium has waxed and waned, infrequently tinkering with my sense of time and space. I have, for instance, occasionally woken up wholly convinced that my hands have enlarged to twice their normal size, a feeling not dissimilar to wearing oven mitts. Other hallucinations can present themselves in a more benign fashion. The solicitor handling my husband's probate and estate administration, for instance, casually mentioned that she smelled her brother's cologne on the first anniversary of his death, an anecdote that brought me back to the basement corridor of the National Hospital for Neurology and Neurosurgery in July 2012. To the day I smelled citrus as I waited for post-operative news outside the recovery bay.

It didn't happen overnight, but over time I have come to accept – and even respect – my disturbances as a cognitive strength, not a weakness. Similar to the sting of my fingers on a burning hot saucepan handle, each one has signalled to me that my senses are alert, that my mind is active, and that my pain is real. We talk a lot about the fragility of grievers, but we rarely discuss their strength. After ten restless nights in Andalucía I was convinced that my mind-expanding insomnia would last forever and that I would never again experience the gentle incurve of sleep, but I was wrong. After seven straight nights of deprivation, something in me shifted, a tiny movement that was partly encouraged by an open letter a friend had texted me as I lay on

Cila's guest bed one afternoon. It was written by the musician Nick Cave in response to a question by a fan about the recent loss of his fifteen-year-old son.

'We are tiny, trembling clusters of atoms subsumed within grief's awesome presence. It occupies the core of our being and extends through our fingers to the limits of the universe. Within that whirling gyre all manner of madnesses exist; ghosts and spirits and dream visitations, and everything else that we, in our anguish, will into existence. These are precious gifts that are as valid and as real as we need them to be. They are the spirit guides that lead us out of the darkness.'

I slept soundly after reading his words. They made me feel less delirious, less mad. Although my sleep would come and go over the next year, the hallucinatory nature of those nights would never return. The mind rebounds, the body takes over, moods fluctuate, seasons change. One minute I was shuffling along a beach promenade in Cádiz and the next I was bustling down familiar pavements back home, bypassing plump Christmas trees huddled outside fairy-lit pubs. I didn't think it was possible but somehow I'd reached mid-December.

My memory between Spain and New Year's Eve is pretty sketchy – even now. Here are a few things I remember. I travelled up to Manchester for a panel event I had been asked to participate in to promote a book of essays I had contributed to. I began working again because I enjoyed the process of editing others' words when I was lost in my own. I framed a couple of Riot Grrrl posters and splattered them on my living room wall. I ticked the option marked *widowed* on my home insurance policy renewal. I laughed a lot. I cried a lot – in offices, at friend's houses, in public toilet cubicles, on park benches. I lost my temper in supermarket queues. I punched a wall. I shouted at a bus driver. I took wedding photographs down and I put them back up again. I bought gig tickets. I sang along to Joni Mitchell as I cooked my dinner. I spoke softly to the birds in our silver birch tree.

I made the decision to return to work in mid-November. As a freelancer, I had been employed as a full-time writer and editor by a women's website called *The Pool* up until my husband's death. When I came back from Spain, my empty flat seemed emptier somehow, and it was certainly darker and colder than it had been in mid-September when the leaves first began to change from jade green to copper. So, I drifted around in *The Pool*'s office, chatting and typing, with a detachedness that helped me compartmentalise his death away from home. Some days when I wandered through Soho's bustling streets, I felt afraid; on other days, I felt tranquil. On one of the last Friday nights before Christmas, I found myself wandering around Topshop in Oxford Circus, dazed yet immersed. I had impulsively cancelled after-work drinks with a good friend at short notice. I was unable to talk, unwilling to engage but neither in my darkened state was I able to handle a packed tube carriage at rush hour. And so the bright lights and pumping music lassoed me in. I was craving anonymity in my grief and I found it here amongst the sequin jumpsuits and festive jumpers, steered by the acetone wafts of shellac nail polish into a conflicted state-of-being.

This splintered approach was actually a perfect way to handle the festive season. Not denial exactly – indifference. I acknowledged its existence but I felt numb to the carol singers and gaudy lights and red-cupped eggnog lattes, paying little attention to the adjunctive existentialism that can disfigure your thoughts at this time. Christmases of yore were always a modest affair in our house, but we never scrimped on the tree. Our first official Christmas together took place five months after his brain surgery but he still insisted on carrying – nay, dragging – the giant fir from our local pub up the high street and around the corner to our living room. I trailed three steps behind them, shouting unhelpful directions as he wheezed and puffed and swore his way past disgruntled shoppers. When he levered its trunk into a stable and upright position, however, he beamed, satisfied with his post-operative accomplishment.

It was the only component to Christmas he really liked, the paganism. A whole subsection of our bookshelf is dedicated to it: folklore, rituals, customs, ceremonies. He once persuaded me to accompany him to Shakespeare's Globe on a chilly Sunday morning in October to watch a Berryman – a man covered head to toe in green paint, foliage, berries and leaves – parade a Corn Queene, a Hobby Horse, and a motley crew of Elizabethan extras through Borough Market in the name of October Plenty, a harvest celebration. I complained, of course I complained, but underneath it all I treasured his inquisitiveness, especially when it came to the strange and the surreal. I mocked and revered it, the precious curiosity in him that both challenged and delighted me.

I couldn't bear to do it in 2018. Buy a tree. I tried, I stood outside our local pub and perused the conifers, but the heady wafts of pine were a trigger scent too far. It felt like a betrayal, to carry on this ritual without him, to retrace his footsteps through our neighbourhood and mimic an experience we had previously shared together. Christmas ornaments weren't just Christmas ornaments, they were painful mementos. Every holiday we ever went on we would try to purchase something to decorate next year's branches, a tradition that began with a shopping trip in Bloomingdale's on a week-long visit to New York. I nabbed a rather glitzy-looking Chrysler Building and from there we kept adding to the collection. A hand-painted folk bauble from a boutique in Krakow. A jointed Pinocchio from a tourist stall in Rome. Each one representing not just one memory, but a swarm of them encased within breakable glass. To decorate a tree now would be to construct a cairn of him out of gaudy tat, a loose rock pile of even looser remembrances, delicately balanced, one by one, in the centre of our living room.

In any case, my mind was elsewhere, 5,545 miles away from here, in fact, rippling in the fresh water springs at the place where flowers grow. I heard a gentle lapping beneath the willow trees and followed its sound. A floating garden, an undulating Eden, elevated high into the thick, smoggy haze.

Part II

WATER

The river is within us, the sea is all about us;
The sea is the land's edge also, the granite
Into which it reaches, the beaches where it tosses
Its hints of earlier and other creation:
The starfish, the horseshoe crab, the whale's backbone;
The pools where it offers to our curiosity
The more delicate algae and the sea anemone.
It tosses up our losses, the torn seine,
The shattered lobsterpot, the broken oar
And the gear of foreign dead men. The sea has many voices,
Many gods and many voices.

– T.S. Eliot, 'The Dry Salvages', *Four Quartets*, 1940–41

FOUR

On New Year's day a boatman's oar sliced into the silken water 17 miles south of Mexico City: a quiet exertion under the surface that gave an illusion of effortlessness as Andy and I glided above. Weaving slowly amongst houses and through wetlands, I spotted an aproned abuelita leaning out from a passing window pegging laundry onto a washing line, and for a brief moment our eyes met before our painted barge passed under a low-lying canal bridge. Shadows relinquished themselves to the dappling light. From here on in, roofs and doorways made way for weeping ferns and towering cypress trees, reflections that fluttered and crinkled below. A moving textile of woven green threads – emerald, sage, moss, teal – that danced to the distant tootles of a mariachi trumpet. It was almost impossible to distinguish land from water here. The flickers of cedar and pine tendrils blended seamlessly into the trees around us, a tapestry of bushy fingertips that reached up into the sky above. Breathing in the sweet, earthy scent of griddled tortillas and corn on the cob, I dangled over the side of our gondola and pattered my fingers into the blue with the words of another running through my head.

'The river is within us, the sea is all about us;'

Some poetry gets under your skin, knitting so seamlessly with your own matter that it is hard to extricate one from the other.

T.S. Eliot wrote 'The Dry Salvages', the penultimate poem of his *Four Quartets*, during the Blitz in 1940–41, quickly penning drafts whilst working night shifts as an air raid warden in South Kensington, a restless poet scouring for flames in a capital that was under siege. Its title, however, reaches further back to his childhood across the Atlantic, a small cluster of rocks off the coast of Cape Ann in Massachusetts, which is where its rhythms flow between the water and the rubble, a 'moment in and out of time'. 'The Dry Salvages' has often been described as a poem of hope, but it is also a cautionary meditation. Eliot's stanzas wrap themselves around the unknowable mysteries of time and ask us to step outside it altogether in order to embrace an expanse with no beginning or end. A liminal space where 'the way up is the way down' and 'the way forward is the way back'.

When my husband asked me to scatter his ashes on the banks of the River Thames, I told him that I planned to return to Mexico, the place where we had holidayed seven years previously. In many ways that trip had bookmarked the start of things. It was both an end and a beginning, our moment in and out of time. On an April evening in 2011, the day before my twenty-eighth birthday, we had sat on a beach north-west of Acapulco, frosty margaritas in hand, gazing at the waves. My sunburned thighs chafed against the plastic seating, but it didn't bother me that night as I buried my toes in the cool sand and watched the sky transform from papaya to cerise to cornflower blue, blushed cheeks tingling from our afternoon rambles through town. I had an inkling tonight might be the night, a hunch that had little to do with any clairvoyance on my part and everything to do with his inability to stick with surprises. He either got too excited or hesitancy set in, and this time round it was the latter, which was entirely understandable given my past insistences that I wasn't the marrying kind.

A month before our holiday he sat opposite me in our local pub and asked how I'd react if someone proposed to me. 'Say, on a beach, for example.' *Was I really adverse to marriage?* 'No, not adverse,' I replied, trying to repress a knowing smile as I did so, 'but not fixated on it, either.'

I had never draped a pillowcase over the back of my head dreaming of my big day, but I had always hoped for love, which to my mind wasn't the same thing. In the years before we met, I had pursued rough affairs with a wildness that armoured my soft, squishy core. When I was a young girl, my mother regularly took me to Tate Britain on rainy Sunday afternoons and, as a result, my notion of love had become a little warped. At a time when most pubescent bedrooms were plastered with Take That posters, my statement wall was an ode to suicidal teenage passion, a mammoth reprint of John Everett Millais' *Ophelia* that I earnestly purchased in my local Athena shop and laminated for posterity. A subsequent deep dive into *Jane Eyre* only confused things further, triggering a decade of annihilation that I now like to call my Mr Rochester Era. In my early twenties I had mistaken love for pain, that ultimate Venus flytrap that nabs so many of us, not with deadly trigger hairs, but with an equally pernicious delusion that if something hurts it's somehow made real.

By the time I met my husband-to-be I was looking for something kinder, something gentler, someone absolute, and I found it in an Italian coffee bar on Frith Street. I should have found it earlier, but our love story wasn't a perfect anecdote – whose is? We had actually met years before our first date, during the mid-noughties, in a lift hurtling towards the twenty-fifth floor of King's Reach Tower, a shabby high-rise building in Southwark that perfectly matched the scruffy goings-on at the *New Musical Express*. I was a freelancing rookie on the magazine's news desk, a Woodstock anomaly with a penchant for flares, Dylan bootlegs and Bukowski poetry – a resolute personal brand that provoked daily wisecracks amongst colleagues in the age of glow sticks and new rave. He was the Associate Editor, a sharply dressed garage rocker whose calm and quiet demeanour belied a renegade passion for avant-garde sounds. Although we worked together for over a year, our paths didn't really cross until after I'd left, burned out by the job and partially gnarled by the rough jaws of an inadequate ex-boyfriend. We sat on high stools in Soho's Bar Italia and drank late-night espressos. The coffee machine whirred and I finally took a breath.

The marriage proposal itself, two years later, on a beach in the small surfing town of Zihuatanejo on the Pacific coast of Mexico, lacked any formality. It was soft and honest and true. Without fuss or fanfare, his body leaned in to whisper something in my ear, a stanza so quiet I could barely catch the words. The ring was made of silver and amethyst, a stand-in for the real thing. He didn't like the idea of picking one out for me, he said. He had tried; he had paced up and down Hatton

Garden's jewellery quarter on a Saturday afternoon pointing at art deco designs in glass cabinets, but it didn't seem right to him. 'What's with all these patriarchal traditions?' he asked. I was the one who would be wearing it every day, so I should be the one to decide what it should look like. That said, he still needed a prop to help him do the asking. He had sneaked into my jewellery box the month before and with a stealthy technique that wouldn't seem out of place in an Agatha Christie novel, moulded a lump of Blu Tack around one of my rings to estimate my finger size.

In the last month of his life, he became fixated on his wedding ring. One morning I walked into his hospice room with an armful of supplies – sausage rolls, lemon drizzle cake, laundry, cans of Guinness – to find him anxiously rummaging through drawers and cabinets looking for it. The white gold band had loosened and he needed to know where it was. Every evening he removed it before he went to sleep. Every morning he asked for it to be brought to him and slid it back onto his ring finger with the same reverence as he had done on our wedding day. Hours after he died, I threaded his wedding band onto an old silver coil necklace. Sliding my thumb through its hoop, I'd often caress its unending line. On the morning I flew to Mexico City, four months later, I reached for the silver and amethyst ring in my jewellery box and placed it ceremoniously onto my right hand before dragging my suitcase up the stairs.

In T.S. Eliot's world, time is both a destroyer and a preserver. When I floated the Mexico idea to Andy I called it a pilgrimage, although I had a limited understanding of what that really meant. I had read about the bathers who wade into the water of the River Ganges in Varanasi, a city in northern India. Pilgrims crowd together on its banks every morning. Facing towards the rising sun, they scoop up handfuls of water with their bare hands and, holding it aloft, release it back again into the blue. The Ganges is a sacred river for Hindus. A celestial body. An incarnation of the goddess Gaṅgā. It is believed that its waters once flowed through the hair of the god Shiva and, even now, this story is remembered and ritualised on its banks. The Manikarnika Ghat is one of the holiest cremation grounds on the Ganges. When a body is cremated here, Hindu pilgrims believe that the soul is freed from the endless cycle of reincarnation. Diana Eck, Professor of Comparative Religion and Indian Studies at Harvard University, quoted in Neil MacGregor's *Living with the Gods*, writes that bathing here is an act of worship:

'When the water is taken up into one's cupped hands and poured back into the river as an offering it is a form of worship. And Ganges is a place for worship on an enormous scale: it just so happens that this particular cathedral is a river.'

It took Andy and me two hours on three different metro trains to reach my watery cathedral in Mexico City. On the first of January, we journeyed nineteen miles from our rented apartment in a leafy northern suburb to the canal district of Xochimilco and bartered with an enterprising boatman moored at the water's edge. Tourists flock to this floating garden every day, queuing up to take magical mystery tours on the brightly painted trajineras that cruise the 110-mile canal system, a shrunken imprint of the vast lake it once was. Pounding the pavements of central Mexico City, with its wide avenues dominated by skyscrapers and office blocks, it seems almost inconceivable that this vibrant and smoggy metropolis, now thronging with a population of 9.2 million people, was once built on water. The Aztecs constructed their city on a vast lake. Even its name flows: the Aztec Nahuatl name for the Valley of Mexico, 'Anahuac', means *land on the edge of water*, and its rhythms still course through its veins, although none of the lake water now remains. The more I've read about the artificial drainage that followed the Spanish conquest of Mexico, to prevent the city from flooding, the more I've come to appreciate the country's losses and its grief. The ghostly indentation of Lake Texcoco has a tale to impart under every pavement slab. Listen quietly and you're sure to hear it.

Xochimilco speaks of its past, too. It ripples and flows. This floating town, nicknamed 'the Venice of Mexico', is home to two rivers, a maze of canal tributaries and what is left of its lake. Its name is a hybrid of the Nahuatl words 'xochitl' and 'milli' meaning *the place where the flowers grow*, and its floating gardens, called chinampas, are still used to grow plants and crops to sell – dahlias, day lilies, corn, radishes, coriander. It is also a place to party. The second our boat curved into the canal's main thoroughfare, our nose rammed with another's tailpiece – a standard altercation on this jammed motorway of revelling Mexicans in carousing boats, some blasting traditional Banda music, others selling flower crowns and spicy micheladas made with sweetened tomato juice, beer and lime. A particularly riotous gondola to the right of us caught my attention and, as I watched four men samba around their beers, I was reminded of the tango dancers my husband and I had stumbled across in Taxco de Alarcón, a rugged town south-west of Mexico City etched into the craggy mountains and cliffs that surround its narrow streets and red-tiled houses. We had stopped there en route to Zihuatanejo, and on a balmy Saturday evening we sat outside a local bar drinking tequila shots with the twirling shadows of zigzagging couples darting across the main square.

I had dressed up that night – a floral skirt with a white ruffled top – and had plaited my hair, pinning it across my head, in a Heidi style, with kirby grips. Strolling around the town's cobbled streets, we dodged speeding VW Beetle taxis, and I stopped every now and then, squeezing his arm enthusiastically as I peered longingly into boutique windows that displayed row upon row of Taxco's traditional, handcrafted silver jewellery: turquoise-studded bangles, Aztec-inspired earrings, garnet and topaz rings. We finally decided on a restaurant, taking a gamble by ordering a plate of grilled prickly pear cactus tacos, smothered with cheese. It was a balmy night and there was a dewiness in the air that curled the thin, wispy hairs that had escaped either side of my pinned-plaits. My cheeks began to glow and I cooled them down with sips of ice-cold beer.

A few hours later we were sitting outside a local bar, drinking tequila shots, watching the animated goings-on that encircled the main square. I remember watching a particularly affectionate couple in their sixties glide across the plaza with a *slow, slow, quick, quick, slow,* and I was instantly transported to the first morning I had woken up in a bed that wasn't mine with a warm, cosy sensation underneath the sheets. I was 26 years old and I hadn't felt that before. I felt it again as I followed the tangoing couple with my eyes, these two scenes in my life, separated by time and place, conjoined in my heart, threaded together by a feeling of belonging.

In the two years between our first date and our Mexican road trip, I began to grow roots. Without even realising, I started to trust my surroundings a bit more. In my early twenties, I had succumbed to things without really choosing them. I wanted to write but I wasn't sure how. I wanted to speak but I questioned the value of what I had to say. I wanted to love but I kept capitulating to men I knew I never really would. I sketched doodles in conference rooms whilst colleagues sounded off assuredly. I wrote short stories I never submitted. I sat silently in a West End pub whilst my soon-to-be-ex-boyfriend cried into his pint because he made me too sad. Which brings us back to those high stools in Bar Italia in 2009. I was desperate for something to change, but I was frustrated because I knew it could only come from me and I didn't know how to bring it about.

A year before my husband and I started dating, I told that soon-to-be-ex-boyfriend that the very things which had attracted him to me were now the very things that were repelling him. I anticipated it, I expected it. Men wanted the fantasy – complicated, flirtatious, smoky-eyed, fork-tongued – and I usually gave it to them, but it wasn't the real me, which confused things further down the line. My husband was the first man I'd ever dated who actually saw through all the artifice. He didn't push, he didn't prod. I was held but I wasn't led. He had the humility to recognise that I wasn't his to shape and mould. My husband and I had more of a *slow, slow, quick, quick, slow* approach to things – and it worked. We found a polyrhythmic groove all of our own. A few weeks after our late-night espresso, I woke to the sound of a whistling kettle on the hob and, although it would take me years to centre myself fully, I felt his sheets brush my skin, and it felt like coming home.

The roots of a word can be hard to unearth. Take 'home', for instance. It is both a physical space and a metaphysical idea. Some people spend their whole lives chasing it. Others are content to remain in the only one they've ever known. I first wrote about my grief in October 2018. 'It is 52 days since my husband passed away,' I announced to readers of *The Pool*. 'I am homesick for him.' Homesickness seemed to be the most accurate word to describe my feral distress at that time; it was like yearning, a longing that took hold of me with such a strength of force that it seemed to disembody me as I floated from one room to the other. I recently discovered that the Welsh word for homesickness is 'hiraeth', which takes on this complexity in a way that the English language can't quite seem to manage. Hiraeth, a multi-layered noun that has as much to do with the past as it does the present and future. A pining for a homeland that you cannot return to, or perhaps an acreage in your heart that only really exists in your imagination. It is a word saturated in loss with no boundaries to pen it in, and as December bowed out to Janus, the god of beginnings and transitions, it was a word I clung to.

I left my home on the cusp of the new year to try to find a way back to myself which, granted, sounds clichéd but some stereotypes are popular for a reason. The concept of a journey might have lost some of its profundity in recent years, diluted by *X Factor* montages and rainbow-hued Instaquotes, but we are all moving creatures whether we like to indulge in the significance of this or not. I could have done an *Eat, Pray, Love*: picked a trio of disparate locations and backpacked through them in order to gain some semblance of inner peace, maybe even bagged myself a Javier Bardem wannabe in the process, but somehow that didn't appeal. I could have shut my eyes and pinned a yellow marker on a random Google Maps spot with my laptop mouse – disrupt the norm, take a chance – but that didn't seem right, either. I felt the water inside me, shoaling and breaking in constant flux, pleading for some kind of reiteration, which is what my trip to Mexico was all about. The act of repeating in order to propel myself forwards, a quest that wasn't just about the past but about my present and future and what that could potentially look like.

I was also seeking reassurance. I needed to show myself that there was a gap between my two selves: the 28 year old who said *yes* on that beach in Mexico and the 35 year old who had wailed *no, no, no* as she kissed the cool, grey skin of her husband's forehead. I had finally experienced the horrifying synchronicity of genuine love and pain, but how far had I really travelled, and was I at risk of regressing back to the woman I had been before I met my husband? Was such a thing possible? I had my doubts, and they kept me awake at night. Whispers that goaded me in the dark with their conjecture. A fear of what *could be*, an uneasiness that my husband had been an anomaly and that, without his steady hand to guide me, the current might pull me away completely.

Sometimes you have to retrace your steps in order to find a new path to the way things are. At my husband's funeral, I shared a memory with the 60-odd congregation of family and friends who were invited to the art gallery where we had been married five years previously, a Palladian villa built in 1710, by the River Thames in Twickenham. I stood in the exact spot where we said *I do* and read out a three-page love letter typed out in Arial font. In the days after his death, my bewildered mind took me back to a location I was never able to show him, but spoke of often, a small nook rooted in the past. My memory was a coastal headland in south-east Cornwall that my family and I visited each year with my grandmother. As a child I would zigzag down the cliff face with wild abandon, my mother nervously calling out to me as I sprinted down the narrow coastal path to the sea.

These were the early years before fear and consequence took hold of me, I told the mourners – before the world sanded down a layer or two. These were the days of excitement, curiosity, faith and adventure. In the years before I met my husband, I had lost some of that fearlessness, drifted a little too far away from the girl on that coastal path, bounding down the steep rock to the sea without any doubt that my spindly legs would get me there. 'The purest partnerships can bring us back to ourselves,' I told them, although that was only half the story, because when a partnership breaks, this repossession does, too.

About a month before he died, I wandered into the park next door to King's College Hospital and sat on a bench near the bandstand. When I swivelled round to adjust my jacket, I glanced at its dedication plaque and read it out loud with memories of Whitsand Bay rustling in the chestnut trees above me. 'St Cecilia, Patron Saint of Singers', it read.

'We can all sing but we have forgotten how.'

In many ways, my second trip to Mexico was bound up in a nostalgia for the past, a term that has loosened and softened over time, but when it was first coined in the late-seventeenth century it was genuinely believed to be a sickness. The Swiss physician Johannes Hofer actually called it a form of grief in his dissertation, portmanteauing this new affliction from two Greek words – 'nóstos', meaning *homecoming*, and 'álgos', meaning *pain* or *ache*. Over the centuries, nostalgia became a medical condition to be treated, not an existential wistfulness to be romanticised. The Swiss doctor Albert Van Holler documented a wide range of symptoms associated with nostalgia including fainting, a loss of appetite, stomach pain and hallucinations. In the eighteenth century, physicians and practitioners even went looking for a nostalgic bone, as if a person's yearning for a distant place, a past you can't quite return to, could be pinpointed to a hunk of tissue. These days, we often speak of nostalgia in terms of waves, similarly to grief itself, which gives this bittersweet pining a tidal movement, a sense of restlessness that is harder to point to on an X-ray lightbox.

Sitting in the departure lounge, with a wide-brimmed hat in one hand and my boarding pass in the other, these waves began to swell again. As I lugged my suitcase through Heathrow airport, niggling doubts resurfaced. Was this a bit nuts? Retracing my steps so exactly that they would take me to the precise spot where I had watched the sun set with my dead husband seven years ago? My mind paced with intrusive thoughts, a Greek chorus of unhelpful bystanders with equally unhelpful questions to ask. *Why are you doing this?* they probed. *To say goodbye*, I replied – a simple answer with multiple meanings because, whilst I was journeying in order to let go of the man I had lost, I was also stepping onto the plane to say farewell to the woman I had been, the 28 year old who said yes on that seashore, which was just as important, perhaps more so.

My husband used to describe memory as mental time travel. Virginia Woolf called it 'a capricious seamstress'. Marcel Proust experienced an involuntary memory when the moistened crumbs of a madeleine invaded his senses on the palate of his tongue. The first thing that hit me when I stepped off the aeroplane in Zihuatanejo, after a quick one-hour flight from Mexico City, was the humidity. It seemed to liquefy my skin, making the freckles on my shoulders ripple and dance. My hair kinked and crimped in the sweltering air that whooshed through me when the cabin crew finally opened the exit door and I shuffled down the airstair onto the hot tarmac below.

They call it sensory memory, the five senses – sight, sound, smell, touch and taste – that can trigger flashes of buried moments from times gone by. When Andy and I stepped off the aircraft, the past caressed my cheeks before enveloping me in an embrace that felt as real to me as any human equivalent. We had spent our first five nights in Mexico City and now we had returned to the centre of things, which was a risky endeavour but I honestly believed that this retracing of steps would release me somehow. That evening we strolled down the tree-lined fisherman's path towards the water's edge, and when the tears came it was the first time I actually felt in command of them.

Only days previously I had been sobbing on a sofa, in a rented apartment in Mexico's capital, at 4am. I hadn't slept for a week – not just a few restless hours either side of slumber but an ocean of wakefulness that left me pining for the magical realism that hallmarked my last insomniatic bout in Spain. At least I could lose myself in those delusions, trick myself that sleep may have occurred somewhere amongst them, but there were no hallucinations this time, despite my attempts to will them into existence. I squinted my eyes at the sharp lines of the wardrobe that loomed on the other side of my bedroom but the panels remained stiff, solid and wooden. Every time I began to sink into unconsciousness my spasming muscles would jolt me out of it with a sudden jerk that caused me to punch the mattress.

I got up. I wandered around the kitchen. I called my mother and she told me that I was brave.

On one of our final nights in Mexico City, before we flew to Zihuatanejo, I withdrew a wad of pesos from an ATM before absent-mindedly wandering off without my debit card. It took me three hours to realise what I had done, by which point we were halfway across the city in a hotel bar and it was too late to retrieve it. *Another lost thing to add to the pile of paraphernalia and memories*, I thought, as I gulped down a margarita.

'It's okay,' Andy said, as he got out his wallet to settle the bill, only it wasn't okay, it was nowhere near okay, and the rage began to intensify as we walked back to our apartment.

Andy's calmness only seemed to make things worse – an unfortunate development that he was only made aware of when we opened the front door and I threw my bag onto the kitchen counter, crying and shouting. I ranted, he listened, standing still as I paced back and forth, from cooker to fridge, handing me the stage in deliberate silence, watching me unravel, because he knew that's what I needed to do. Because it wasn't about the debit card and we both knew it. I was angry at the cancer, I was angry at the 999 calls, I was angry at the underwear in his sock drawer, the sympathetic head tilts and the endless paperwork that was still waiting for my return – and I had no idea where to aim my rage. So I hurled it against the wall instead.

On the first evening that we reached Zihuatanejo, I swallowed a couple of melatonin pills and prayed to my own body for it to release me. Over the next week, sleep returned, slowly, cautiously – from four hours to six and then, finally, eight – as if it had been patiently waiting for the roar and crash of the sea. Its rhythms soothed and softened me. The breaking waves mirrored the wild bellows I felt inside. We were staying with friends of my parents, in a condominium that backed on to a large swimming pool which I swam in most days – occasionally in the morning, but usually in the mid-afternoon when the sweltering heat proved too much for me, dipping my sticky body into the cool water with a slosh and a sigh.

'You look very graceful when you do that!' a retired Canadian expat remarked as she sat at a nearby table drinking a glass of wine. She had been watching me for some time, glancing over every now and then as I spread my arms like angel wings under the surface, fluttering my feet every so often to keep my torso afloat. I didn't have the heart to tell her that my swimming style had little to do with graceful technique and everything to do with my lack of proficiency and skill. It had taken me over a year to get my 10-metres swimming certificate as a child, and floating like this, as a serene sea otter might do on its back, was the only way of disguising this inaptitude. That said, I did feel pretty tranquil doing it, drifting and floating whilst I looked up at blue skies and green palms, my ears muffled by the *whoosh* of my own body in the water – as light as polystyrene, as heavy as stone.

A few nights before our return flight to Mexico City, Andy and I sauntered to a restaurant called La Sirena Gorda – translated as The Fat Mermaid – and recreated the meal I had eaten on the night my husband and I got engaged: blackened red snapper with dollops of tangy guacamole and salty tortilla chips. After that, we ordered potent margaritas from a nearby bar and walked them onto the beach. I kicked off my sandals and lay down on the cool sand, tracing unknown constellations with my fingertips between salty sips of lime and orange. Sight, sound, smell, touch and taste. I had missioned it halfway around the world to feel them all, an act of pilgrimage that has been attempted by so many heartbroken explorers before me.

Fifty years after his father died in 1731, the writer Samuel Johnson returned to his hometown in Staffordshire and stood alone in the market square 'bareheaded, in the rain, on the spot where my father's stall used to stand' – a delayed act of repressed grief that is remembered with a special ceremony each year in the West Midlands market town by its residents, who call it 'Johnson's Penance'. A few months after my father-in-law passed away, my husband walked to the grave of Sandy Denny, lead singer of the British folk rock band Fairport Convention, in Putney Vale Cemetery – a secular pilgrimage that enabled him to emote all the things he had been unable to by his father's side. In 2017, I read a news story about the grieving father of a teenager, who embarked on a 560-mile journey along the Camino de Santiago, a network of pilgrims' ways in north-western Spain, in order to relocate her in his mind.

For the writer and theologian C.S. Lewis, the notion of time was an enigma he struggled to decode after the loss of his wife in 1960. A remote landscape so discombobulating that it caused him to question the very foundations of his Christian faith. When religion failed him, he wrote passionately in his journal, an introverted act of pilgrimage that sought to understand the meaning of eternity when it is juxtaposed with only four years of marriage. 'What does *now* mean?' he asks in his meditative treatise, *A Grief Observed*. 'If the dead are not in time, or not in our sort of time, is there any clear difference, when we speak of them, between *was* and *is* and *will be*?'

Inspired by Lewis, I kept an intermittent journal that I unimaginatively called *A Grief Observed #2*. A yellow envelope is nestled between the cover and the first page, inside which is a brittle pressing of a violet wildflower that I picked from the riverbank on the afternoon I ate sauerkraut and mash two days after his death. 'And so, I guess, this is grief,' it begins in ghost-like pencil. (It would take me a few more pages to shift to the permanence of a biro.) 'Horizon out of view. A gentle rocking in a row boat as the water slops over the sides and a damp feeling creeps over my forehead.'

A horizon perfectly suits that opening page. It is a clearly defined boundary and yet it is also hazy and vague, creating a perspective that ultimately eludes us. If you were to look at the earth's surface at an altitude of hundreds of miles from space, our borderline between earth and sky actually appears as a convex arc. The periphery between the living and the dead isn't that different. Looking down at a drawer of underwear and socks was one thing. Fishing each item out and putting them into a bin bag was quite another. It was dirty work and I felt shameful doing it – as if I were dumping and discarding the man and not his earthly garments. When death removed all sense of time and place, my perspective bowed, my gaze shifted. Rocketed through the atmosphere, I orbited an infinite place that was beyond measure. A peculiar swathe of carbon black that had no discernible edge or form. That's where the guilt lies.

If certain events in our life can separate us from the people we once were, then it follows that the spaces in between can bring us closer to the people we're yet to be. I jetted half-way across the world to move a millimetre towards her – that unknown woman ahead of me, that girl on the coastal path light years behind – one tiptoe forwards, another tiptoe back. I guess you could call it a midway point between *was* and *will be*. In anthropology, it even has a name. Liminality is a threshold, a state of transition that was first coined by the Belgian folklorist Arnold van Gennep, who identified this period of disorientation as a fundamental phase of any rite of passage. Liminal periods, van Gennep contended, had to be destructive as well as constructive to initiate change, a metamorphosis that can be triggered by painful moments such as death, divorce or illness which he called 'patterns of living'. As he concluded in his 1909 publication *Rites de Passage*:

'For groups, as well as for individuals, life itself means to separate and to be reunited, to change form and condition, to die and to be reborn. It is to act and to cease, to wait and rest, and then to begin acting again, but in a different way.'

On a balmy evening in early January, I sat on the trampoline netting of a stationary catamaran and watched the yellow and orange light dapple the sparkling water that stretched outwards towards the smudged horizon, disappearing into it, merging seamlessly into the powder-blue sky. *If my husband was still moving between two worlds*, I thought to myself, *then perhaps I was, too.* As one member of the crew shuffled John Lennon's 'Imagine' onto the boat's stereo, another ruffle-haired sailor handed me a shot of tequila. I knocked it back in one and looked out across the immense swathe of salt water, skimming over the velvety crinkles and pleats of the Pacific Ocean, squinting ahead to the burning disc of coral that hovered over it like a giant stick of lollypop. *He hated this song*, I thought to myself, watching the sun dissolve into the water – a trick of the senses *as we are the ones who are moving*, I thought, even on this motionless boat. The waves rocked the hull from side to side, and I felt every rise and fall.

My counsellor once suggested that I was mourning two deaths. The passing of my husband was the obvious one, but the death of myself, or at least a part of myself, was a more complex supposition. It would take me some time to sever one from the other. Google the words 'dolphin' and 'grief' and you will see this rite of separation in action. In 2019, a frantic mother was filmed nudging and cajoling her dead calf through the water in Florida. It is a phenomenon that has also been witnessed in New Zealand, southern China and Greece. In 2017, a bottlenose dolphin was filmed caressing and prodding her baby through the choppy waves of the Ambracian Gulf in western Greece, a frenzied display of grief that marine biologists interpreted as a disorientated mother's attempt to bring her dead child back to life. I have watched this footage many times, over and over, as if this mournful creature was demonstrating something I was unable to vocalise to family and friends – my own struggle to let go of him in the water.

It is the greatest of concessions, the moment when you finally consent to death. I watched my husband slowly acquiesce to it in his hospice bed, but it would take me longer to follow his lead and accept his departure without any thoughts of a fantastical return. We had finally reached a fork in our union that saw us embark on two separate trajectories. One was bound for the world of the dead, and the other had to choose the world of the living.

C.S. Lewis wrote that passionate grief doesn't bind us to the dead, it cuts us off from them. Maybe that's the way it is supposed to be – and perhaps the stories we tell ourselves in this passionate grief are designed to lessen the guilt of such a severance. I also wonder whether we mythologise our pain in order to sanctify it in some way. Maybe it helps us better understand ourselves, but maybe we do it to create a transparent layer between us and reality, like laminate on poster art, because it makes it easier to live with. A heartbroken dolphin in the water. A doomed Russian socialite who throws herself onto the tracks. Elegant Ophelia scattered with poppies on the surface of the Hogsmill River. Fetishisations that spin injury and struggle into something beautiful.

Millais instructed his 22-year-old model, Lizzie Siddal, to lie in a bathtub fully clothed in order to paint his masterpiece. On one of his final composition days, she posed in the cold water for so many hours that her limbs went numb, she caught a chill, and her father charged him £50 for the distress. I didn't discover this detail until I was well into my twenties, by which time the myth had already woven itself into my imagination. I like to think that if I had known earlier it might have tilted my perspective, shifted the theoretical horizon, altered that bedroom wall of mine, but if we're being realistic, and realism is what I'm endorsing, I suspect it wouldn't have changed a thing.

FIVE

A few months after my husband died, an old friend of his emailed me from her home in San Diego with pictures of their Day of the Dead altar attached. Her kitchen table was festooned with multicoloured papel picado skulls and vibrant marigold flowers. A plate of fruit sat in the centre, flanked on either side by pastries and bottles of drink. Behind a scattering of veladoras candles, a colonnade of framed relatives formed an interweaving arch of remembered souls. A photograph of my husband was displayed on the mantelpiece above, propped up against an old copy of the *New Musical Express*, lovingly placed between a porcelain figurine of the Virgin Mary and a black and white photograph of a woman in 1950s attire, possibly a grandmother.

'In our tradition, our friends and family who have departed come back November 1st departing November 2nd,' she wrote. 'We offer them their favorite foods, drinks, etc. etc., so that they enjoy their stay with us that evening. I just wanted to send you a photo and hope that he shows up to have a little party with us.'

I encountered the concept of the Day of the Dead – in Spanish, Día de Muertos – on my first trip to Mexico in 2011. I did what most clueless tourists do. I bought a handful of tin decorations in a local crafts market – a hot pink and turquoise Lady of Guadalupe and a blood red and blue skeleton plaque

– without any real understanding of their complex cultural symbolism. I was pulled in by the vibrant colours and the joyous glint of the metalwork, thinking that they'd look cool on my bedroom wall. It wasn't until I stood in front of the artist Diego Rivera's 1947 mural *Dream of a Sunday Afternoon in Alameda Central Park* that I began to join up the dots. It was a hot and sticky morning in Mexico City and as I stood in front of the giant panorama, fanning myself with a folded museum leaflet, a random gentleman struck up a conversation and offered to guide me through the work – a vast ticker tape of jovial fete-goers, or at least that's how I had envisioned the 51- by 15-foot wall.

How wrong I was. Rivera's surreal vision is actually a sprawling tapestry that charts Mexico's history from the fall of the Aztec Empire to the bloody violence of the Mexican Revolution in the early twentieth century. My companion told me that the balloons and feathers and flags tease us with Mexico's losses: the vast territory that now makes up the United States of California, Nevada, Utah, most of Arizona, half of New Mexico, a quarter of Colorado and a chunk of Wyoming. Holding hands with an infant Rivera, dressed in short trousers and a straw boater, is a towering skeleton wearing a feathered serpent boa and an elaborate Edwardian hat. Her name is La Calavera Catrina, my guide told me, the iconic image of death in Mexico. Rivera immortalised her after spotting a zinc etching made by the Mexican political printmaker José Guadalupe Posada in the early 1900s. Posada's original description nicknames her 'Garbancera', a moniker given to indigenous Mexicans who began wearing European style clothes and, in so doing, denied their own cultural heritage – or at least, that was Posada's take.

Rivera adopted the striking image of Catrina and transformed her into a macabre idol that is now a popular image throughout Mexico. You find her everywhere, a satire on the universality of death and the transience of life. Her clenched grin laughs at it and her colourful clothes flirt with its inevitable pull, for no one is immune to its magnetic force. She embraces the afterlife with the exuberance of her Aztec predecessors who worshipped Mictēcacihuātl, Queen of the underworld, Lady of the Dead, who safeguards the bones of her mortal subjects with her mouth open to swallow the stars.

La Catrina and I share a name, but I also think we share a sensibility. On the morning of my husband's funeral, I put on some crimson lipstick and zipped my feet into a pair of ruby-red boots, defiant sartorial choices that subconsciously sparred with my new status. Yes, they said, I had chosen to be a 30-year-old bride, but I hadn't asked to be this 35-year-old widow.

Weeks later, I hosted a wake at his favourite pub in Central London. Whilst friends and family engaged in quiet and thoughtful conversation, I spun drunkenly on the dance floor as Andy played Stax classics and freakbeat hits. The mourning conventions rankled me and I wasn't playing ball. Not that anyone said anything that afternoon which particularly riled me. In fact, everyone seemed to understand my changeable moods and offbeat choices. There seemed to be a general consensus that whatever I did was whatever I needed to do. I am forever grateful to the hundred-odd mourners at the Betsey Trotwood pub who left me to hustle on the dance floor without pulling me out of my disturbed revelry or making me feel self-conscious about it.

That said, there was an element of defiance at play that day, a resistive attitude that seemed to go against what I believed to be certain stereotypes of how a grieving woman should behave, even how she should dress. Picture Queen Victoria in her sombre black robes, a timeless image that, centuries later, we still refer to when talking about death, grief and widowhood. When her husband, Prince Albert, died in 1861 it sent her into a deep depression that she never fully recovered from, initiating a 'cult of grief' that Richard Brilliant, author of *Death: From Dust to Destiny*, calls 'active mourning'.

She grieved for him by wearing black for the remaining 40 years of her life, avoiding public appearances and comfort eating to the point of excessive weight gain, a state of perpetual mourning and self-flagellation that earned her the nickname 'The Widow of Windsor'. In one photograph, dated towards the end of her life, her puffy face looks down dejectedly at the floor, nervous hands interlaced at her lap, drowning under layer upon layer of black silk taffeta and crepe. When I look at her wearied body I am reminded of the historical rituals of widowhood that I read about at the Wellcome Library in the winter of my grief. An eighteenth-century painting illustrating the ancient practice of sati in South Asia. The 'good wife' who submits herself to the flames of her husband's funeral pyre in order to die alongside him, a horrifying funeral practice that has since been banned in India.

During the Victorian era, mourning became a performance as well as a manifestation of loss, especially for a widow who was simultaneously expected to carry out the duties of her gender. The first stage, full mourning, where a woman wore sombre dress and was socially excluded for a year and a day. The second stage, a period that generally lasted for nine months, where a woman was banned from attending gatherings such as Sunday mass, concerts and weddings. And the third stage, a so-called 'half-mourning', where colour was gradually reintroduced back into her wardrobe. The etiquette for widowers, on the flip side of the coin, lasted between three to six months.

I wouldn't say that my rebelliousness was always a conscious action, but I do think that I was aware of all the customs and conventions that I felt at odds with. If you were to have asked me, on that weekday morning, when I headed into town and hand-picked a pair of red stiletto boots to wear to my husband's funeral, why I had picked them out, I'm sure I would have shrugged and simply said, *Why not?* Looking back, I now realise that there was more to this sartorial choice than met the eye. I was, in fact, sending a clear signal out into the world, a reminder that I was independent from what was happening to me. Granted, my options were limited in those early days, but the ones I had, I seized.

Funeral styling aside, it wasn't until I returned from my Mexican pilgrimage that I really began to tussle with my new title. I read about a widow called Loretta de Braose who, upon the death of her husband in the early thirteenth century, withdrew from everything she knew to live as an anchoress in a church cell in Canterbury – a living death that she forfeited herself to until her actual death 45 years later. I also mused on the sexist stereotypes that I had passively absorbed on my television screen growing up in the 1990s. The voiceless and beautiful Scottish Widow, dewy-eyed and cloaked in black, calmly leading us out of the maze. There is a mysticism to widowhood. She quietly courts our gaze. Cast your mind back to Jackie Kennedy veiled in black on the steps of the United States Capitol in 1963, a silent image that we have appropriated to exalt an impossible ideal, the dignity of the grieving widow.

Its etymology grated on me, too. In Hebrew, the word for widow is 'almanah', from the root 'alem', meaning *unable to speak*. Its Indo-European origin is *to be empty*. And yet, when I looked at my engagement ring and wedding band, a duo of remembrances I reassigned from left hand to right upon my return from Mexico City, I felt neither hollow nor mute, but anxious to move and bursting with life. To anyone who asked, I was very honest about my frustrations. I didn't want to smooth over what was happening and I didn't see why I should subscribe to a role that I hadn't signed up for. I was angry. I felt abandoned, too. To add insult to injury, I couldn't even lob these painful feelings at the person who had left me behind. Believe me, I tried. I quarrelled with my husband at inopportune times, usually when something hadn't quite gone my way – when my coat got jammed in the door, for instance, or when I spilled my morning coffee. Who knows, maybe Jackie Kennedy did too.

The grief myth is a gendered one. No woman wants to be deemed a hysterical mess, especially in widowhood. There are other adjectives, too – *over-emotional, irrational, out-of-control*. One might consider the age of morose queens and incarcerated anchoresses to be a distant one, but even I had my doubts as to how far I could push the envelope, especially as time moved on and people started to ask me questions like, *Do you still think about your husband a lot?* and offered me words of encouragement like, *You're doing so well; the worst is over*. Although well meaning, these kind of queries and statements made me feel like I was now expected to smooth out my kinks. Only, I didn't want to, and the worst wasn't over – it was still ahead of me, it was all around me, miles of ocean that slurped and sloshed against the flimsy hull of my tin-can boat.

On the days that my emotions got the better of me – which, five months down the line, was still a fairly frequent event – I found that my sadness was easier for others to deal with than my anger and irritability, the storm raging within. One could argue that emotional autonomy has always been a battleground in terms of equality and you don't have to look too far into history to see the subtle and not-too-subtle ways that this plays out. Emotional women make us feel uncomfortable. Take the singer Courtney Love, for instance. I don't think I could come up with a better example of how gender plays into grief when a woman refuses to hide her scars. I recently watched the grainy, handheld footage of what many still categorise as her infamous appearance at Reading Festival in 1994, a performance that every commentator likes to point out was *four months after Kurt Cobain's death*, as if by simply stating this time period as fact it sidesteps any judgement. Love, like me, a widow in her early thirties, struts onto the stage in a golden, satin, bias-cut frock that looks like a yellowing wedding dress, slashed to her thighs to release the demons.

'Oh yeah, I'm so brave,' she drawls. 'Let's pretend it didn't happen,' before launching into her set.

One reviewer called the performance 'macabre' and 'frightening'. Another labelled it 'vulgar' and 'offensive'. I call it heroic. When I watch Love pound and pummel her guitar, I don't see a widow who is embarrassing herself at a time when she should be hiding herself away, I see an honest woman who is hurting and is unafraid to show that to the world.

In lieu of an actual stage, my platform was all around me. I wasn't just grieving for an isolated death that occurred in the early hours of 24 August 2018. I was grieving for the years we had spent negotiating with an illness that rarely met us halfway. I was grieving for the months I had watched my husband's dazzling brain guzzle itself as his limbs grew weak and his hands rattled and shook. I wasn't just angry at the death itself, I was angry at the dying I witnessed. The process of losing a person, bit by bit, a disintegration that continues even after the heart stops beating, as cell membranes break down, followed by the tissue and the blood cells and the broken vessels, into gas, into liquid, into salt.

Where do you put that kind of anger? It isn't a solid object you can handle and mould. It moves like mercury; a slithering, quicksilver emotion that liquefies your body into quivering tributaries that pulse and flow. Some days it seemed to seep through my nerves and capillaries until it was trickling on the surface of my skin, crawling down my shoulders and arms. On a weekday morning, I met my mother in town, and when she tried to embrace me, I physically recoiled from her with a jerk and a push of my hand, as if to touch me would be to dip into me, to plunge into my pain – a fluid sensation I wasn't willing to share.

It was often a battle to protect my husband, especially in those final weeks, struggling to help him die as peacefully as possible when his brain tumour was both savage and cruel. In his final week, I wheeled him down to the hospice gym and watched him from the doorway as he pumped his biceps using an arm bike, only his arms no longer moved, and the motion was a barely perceptible tug that he nonetheless kept repeating, again and again and again.

When Dame Cicely Saunders established the world's first modern hospice in south-east London, she did so based on the following mission statement: 'You matter because you are you, and you matter to the end of your life. We will do all we can not only to help you die peacefully, but also to live until you die.' When my husband and I arrived at St Christopher's Hospice, I drew back the curtains of his room and took in the view of Crystal Palace Park. We were both beleaguered and grateful to finally be somewhere private and quiet. He had spent a fortnight on a raucous general ward which was stuffy and loud and he had barely slept. His previous roommate, a babbling 50 year old with severe learning difficulties, rocked and moaned throughout the night, begging to return to a home that didn't exist, pleading to an audience that wasn't there.

I had very little knowledge of what hospices really did before my husband checked in to one. How many of us can honestly say that we do? We fear the things we cannot see. Palliative care is too often described as invisible work. It is carried out in tucked-away corners of our society, away from the humdrum of everyday life, siphoned off, out of sight, out of mind. I remember visiting my grandmother in a hospice that was named after Saint Raphael, patron saint of the sick and the displaced. I was nine years old and disorientated. My grandmother was, too. When I wandered into her hospice room she immediately shouted for me to leave, angry, not at me, but at the disease itself, angry at its pace, angry at its might, angry at its supremacy.

Twenty-six years later, I recognised this same anger in myself, but I suppressed it and swallowed it down. For an entire year after my husband died I kept certain truths to myself, uneasy at speaking them out loud, afraid of how others might perceive things. His death, my grief. One of the last things he said to me took so much effort for him to actualise that it cleaved me in two. 'This isn't momentous,' he whispered. Three words, plainly spoken, a statement not just on the expectations we all have of life, but on the hopes we pin on death as well. The expectation we have for that moment to mean something. I didn't have it in me to tell people the truth, to recall his clenched fists punching the mattress because he had an appalling headache and the morphine wasn't working. I didn't have the strength to concede that despite all our hopes and expectations, sometimes it's a headache that pushes us over the line.

In Mexico there is a saying that goes: 'In this painful world nobody escapes from death.' I find this a strangely soothing aphorism in spite of its morbidity. Game recognises game, as they say. I'm a pretty direct person, sometimes a little too forthright for my own good, so it felt reassuring to discover an entire population that is just as brassy. There is a wildness to the Mexican approach to dying and loss that matched my own and offered me companionship at a time when my inner world felt far too unruly to be considered rational. If they could break down the fourth wall between the living here, and the dead over there, then why couldn't I?

As Carmichael and Sayer write in their explorative book, *The Skeleton at the Feast: The Day of the Dead in Mexico*:

'To the inhabitant of New York, Paris or London, death is a word that is never uttered because it burns the lips. The Mexican, on the other hand, frequents it, mocks it, caresses it, sleeps with it, entertains it; it is one of his favourite playthings and his most enduring love.'

When you find yourself surreptitiously joking with your dead husband, as I often did, you start looking for alternative narratives, especially if you're grieving in an environment where death is often met with a cock of the head and an uncomfortable pause. One evening at a house party, I bumped into an old friend who, after listening to my prosecco-soaked account of widowhood, peppered with pithy one-liners, tilted her head and stroked my hair with an aura of maternal concern, a natural reflex that although spurred by good intentions, irritated me.

Much like those red boots I purchased for my husband's funeral, my sarcastic wisecracking was a way to reclaim and assert myself, but it was also used to challenge others' traditionalism. I dished out humorous ad libs whenever I could, especially at points in the conversation where concern seemed to tip over into pity, although not always; sometimes I did it to hook myself out from the pit I was in. During a group WhatsApp conversation with two close friends, I used the trending hashtag *#sadnessinhereyes* in order to guilt one into leaving her work drinks early so she could meet us in the pub instead.

Little quips helped me wrestle back some control – not just over my grief but others' responses to it. Like the evening I turned up wearing my new leopard-print dress with slits down the thighs and a nipped-in waist. 'I'm channelling Raquel Welch,' I deadpanned to my friends, knowing full well that this was a performative lie, because to successfully channel Raquel Welch and pull off this panthera look I would need to feel a joie de vivre. In reality, this animal-print outfit was just another costume I was trying out in order to rebrand myself, like the velvet minidress I panic-bought before a Friday night cocktail session with my work colleagues. I stood in a packed bar and went through the motions. I laughed and chatted and swigged down negronis, but I wasn't really in the room because no four walls could have contained me at that time. There were some days that I couldn't even contain myself. When I went to pay for my cocktails that night, a few casually flirtatious remarks with the barman led to a stroke of my shoulder and I thwacked it away before storming out in tears. I wished to be seen, I wanted to disappear, and at no point could I ascertain which version of myself I wanted to be.

I thought everyone could see the sadness. On a weekday morning I stood in the changing room of a Lee jeans store in Covent Garden, clutching nervously at my waistband as a chatty shop assistant leaned against the mirror. Unbeknown to me I had called my reflection 'funny' a couple of times and he wanted to know why. 'What's so funny about the way you look?' he teased. A throwaway line to him, but an existential question for me, and one I couldn't possibly answer. I didn't even know why I had walked into this shop to begin with. And yet in this brief, trivial moment, I wanted to purge myself. Tell this stranger everything, absolutely everything. Rant and shout and rave. Blurt out that, when I looked at the glass surface, all I could see was jagged shapes and crude lines with gritted teeth, triangular tears and mismatched eyes. A grotesque abstraction that I somehow had to reassemble like a 1,000-piece jigsaw puzzle.

Some days I avoided my reflection, other days I confronted it head-on. I would stand in the bathroom and peer into my grandmother's oval mirror, the one I inherited, the one that used to hang on her bedroom wall, a sweet sixteen gift from her mother, that journeyed with her from Plymouth to Gdańsk to London. When I looked into the glass, memories of her washed over me. I remembered staring at my grandmother's hands when I was a child, marvelling at the way that the skin rippled and marbled over her knuckles, the geology of a life lived. There was wisdom there, in her pleats and folds, they told a story. What was mine? I was only 35 years old and I could see the same furrows across my face, except they didn't make sense here. I had no respect for the dark shadows that wreathed under my eyes or the ribbons of silver that streaked through my hair. They didn't honour a life lived, they were the markings of a life lost, and every morning they seemed to goad me as I applied 'instant radiance' concealer to cover them up. Acknowledging these markings was the first step in repossessing myself. The second took me a little further afield.

It may sound superficial, but my healing began in high-street fitting rooms. Denim miniskirts, body-clinging wrap dresses, crocodile-effect ankle boots, bell-sleeved crop tops – I tried them all. I squeezed myself into flared jumpsuits and I dived into fur-trimmed dressing gowns. All bets were off, I was open to anything. It wasn't even about purchasing things so much as experimenting with my reflection in an anonymous space where I could be anyone. Joyce Carol Oates once likened a grieving widow to an inflated balloon. 'The wounded individual, the widow, has been disembodied,' she writes. 'She must try very hard to summon forth the lost "self" – like one blowing up a large balloon, each morning obliged to blow up the large life-sized balloon, the balloon that is you.' The problem with this temporary coping mechanism is that it takes a lot of puff and you have no idea what shape you're going to end up with.

When my sister and I were children, a balloon artist approached us at a birthday party and asked us for a request. My older sibling calmly ordered a shark.

'I can't do that,' he answered.

'But you said you could make anything,' she replied.

I thought about this exchange on the day I grabbed a fringed minidress from a high-street rail and shimmied in it in front of a full-length mirror. Was I turning into some kind of grief shark? Was I trying to stretch and inflate myself into something that was impossible to create? I couldn't even tell anymore, but it beat the alternative. It was better than standing in my bedroom, staring at my husband's wardrobe, skimming through corduroy jackets and Fred Perry polo shirts, breathing in his scent.

I had tried to do it – bag up a lifetime's accumulation of his shirts and ties – but it felt so wrong. When the tributes poured in, everyone cited his slick Ivy League style because he was always so impeccably dressed. Picture George Peppard in *Breakfast at Tiffany's* wearing a skinny tie and pin, or an off-duty John F. Kennedy in tapered chinos and white sneakers. How was I supposed to do this exactly, pull each carefully curated item off the hanger and chuck them into shopping bags? Then what – drop them off at my local charity shop and watch them price up each piece, ready for someone else to animate the lifeless sleeves and floppy legs like some kind of perverted taxidermy?

No, I thought. Better to preserve the cemetery than dig up the graves.

My own wardrobe, however – that was an entirely different matter. I needed to exorcise the past and I did this by culling my clothes. I rifled through dresses and skirts and built a bedraggled mound in the middle of my bedroom, a funeral pyre of cotton and polyester that triggered painful memories and flashbacks I was desperate to forget. When I looked down at the floor, I realised that each garment had been purchased in the last few years of our life together, a life that had been infiltrated by a succession of traumas. Clonic seizures, chemotherapy, memory loss, an unexpected pregnancy followed by a protracted miscarriage. Lost things. Hopeful gambles. Fleeting chances.

One of the most disturbing by-products of the brain tumour was the epilepsy, because we never knew when it was going to spasm and erupt like an explosive geyser. If you've never witnessed a grand mal seizure, I envy you. It is harrowing to watch, it is horrifying to remember. I can still feel the firm grasp of his hand on my shoulder at the supermarket check-out. The recognisable grey pallor on his face giving me my thirty-second warning. The next part I called *following the flying bird*, a semi-circular eye roll from bottom left to top right as his legs crumpled down towards the ground and his body fell like a heavy sack of potatoes. I'm almost ashamed to admit the next bit because it was a pretty primal and self-serving emotion, a desperate feeling of panic and abandonment. One minute he had been helping me to line up the groceries on the conveyor belt, and the next he was unconscious on the floor, I was on my own, and it was up to me to keep him safe. The only problem with this was that each seizure was so different. This one was particularly disturbing because his convulsions were so violent and because his teeth clenching seemed to be preventing him from breathing. *Don't die in this supermarket aisle*, I urged him in my head. *Not here, you're better than this.* Three minutes can feel like 30 hours. A sudden jerk and a leap into the living.

One evening in a bustling bar at the British Film Institute, he jumped to his feet and ran into a glass window. On another, he sprang up from our living room floor with no memory of who I was, or where we were, and when I tried to keep him still he lunged at me, pushed me against a wall, picked up a three-foot wooden doorstop, and chased me out of the house. It wasn't something we talked about a lot – the seizures, the memory loss, the lack of basic recognition. When he reached for his wallet on the supermarket floor I had to explain to him what a wallet was. When he lurched at me on that Friday night, he honestly believed that I was an intruder who had broken in and he responded like a frightened man in mortal danger. How could I dwell on something like that when it caused him so much shame and pain? We were both traumatised in different ways. You learn to adapt, you try to forget, you endeavour to cope. I learned to crouch down on my hands and knees at exactly the right time, to make myself small, and when he finally came back to me I would introduce myself to him like a nursery school teacher might engage with an anxious child.

'Don't be scared – my name is Kat and I'm here to help you.'

'Kat? That name sounds familiar,' he replied. 'I know you are – and I'm incredibly grateful.'

He was the gentlest man I ever met, and in these desperate moments, that gentleness unfurled from the very core of his being like pristine sails.

There are moments, even now, when a flash of sensory stimuli triggers something in me – a sudden burst of adrenaline and then it's gone. Just the other day I wandered into the kitchen and when a flash of blue light dappled onto the floor, projected through the window from a lorry outside, I was back in 2015 waiting for the ambulance to ring the bell. It is hard to trust your body when it can trick you like this. It makes you doubt yourself. It causes you to question what you see reflected back at you.

When I returned from Mexico in mid-January, I began to seek kinship in the bodily estrangement of others. I read about the chronic endometriosis that brutally plagued the writer Hilary Mantel in her early twenties. We can become foreign to ourselves, she writes in her memoir, *Giving Up the Ghost* – through illness, trauma or hormonal imbalance. When the two-time Booker winner finally had a hysterectomy, at the age of 27, her very selfhood had to be painstakingly reimagined and reconstructed, piece by piece, sentence by sentence. 'There are other people who, like me, have had the roots of their personality torn up,' she muses. 'You need to find yourself, in the maze of social expectation, the thickets of memory: just which bits of you are left intact?'

The writer Ariel Levy called herself a missing person. Lost things are replaceable, but what do you do when the life you imagined bleeds out before your eyes? In 2012, she flew to Mongolia to report on the country's mining boom and what it signalled for women. Levy was 38 years old and five months pregnant at the time and was seeking one last adventure before motherhood grounded her for the next few years. When she woke up in her hotel bed on the first day of her assignment, she felt a pain in her abdomen. Hours later, she miscarried her son on the bathroom floor.

'Grief is a world you walk through skinned, unshelled,' she writes in her memoir, *The Rules Do Not Apply*. 'A person would speak to me unkindly – or even urgently – on the street or in an elevator, and I would feel myself ripping apart, the membrane of normalcy I'd pulled on to leave the house coming undone.'

It felt peculiar at first – to identify so absolutely with one woman's account of postpartum grief. But over time, it began to make sense to me. We create invisible lines to make logical divisions between types of loss when the experience itself is anything but. Some of my most profound conversations have occurred with one of my best friends who has contemplated taking her life several times and yet, in her darkest moments, she has found a way to pinpoint the light and reach towards it. She gets my language – and I get hers. Grief isn't static and it has no borders. We don't always grieve for the things we can see. When I read about Levy's bewildered wanderings in a shopping mall, struggling to find clothes to fit a bump without a baby, it brought me back to my Friday night Topshop wanderings amongst the sequins and miniskirts. It hit a nerve. When you feel like a stranger trapped inside your own body, when you no longer recognise its shape and form, how can you possibly find the right clothes to dress it?

Come to think of it, how can you summon the desire to feed it? When you lose your appetite for life it translates to food, which in turn, impacts the body. Mine waxed and waned, and in the immediate months after my husband's death, it shrank to such a degree that it alarmed those around me. 'Are you eating enough?' friends would frequently ask as I forced down smoothies at their request. Many more of them hand-delivered Tupperware containers filled with home-cooked meals, door-stop takeaways that I stacked at the back of the fridge alongside a four-pack of Guinness that my husband had left behind. I couldn't even tell you which seemed the sadder sight. I snipped open freezer bags of ragù and did my best to play along, gulping down enough mouthfuls to keep me upright – no more, no less. Cheeks hollowed and jeans sagged. Friends increasingly began to express concern.

'Just eat this bit and then we'll go to the gig,' Andy instructed me, portioning out a small section of rice and pulled pork at a Mexican restaurant in Central London.

These sorts of exchanges happened regularly. My appearance was the only visible indicator the outside world had to go on and so my body became subject to a very public dialogue; my weight was a focal point, something for others to sustain and protect – which is a totally understandable reaction and one that I imagine is very common in this kind of scenario. But what happens when the body returns to its former shape and that indicator is no longer there? What then?

There was a dissonance between my body and my head, between my public and private worlds, and I hopped from one to the other, switching and swapping from one day to the next. On the one hand, I needed my grief to be seen and acknowledged. I craved others' care, I wanted their attention. And yet, on the other, I would often try to disguise or conceal it because that was the only way I could begin the process of remaking myself anew.

February and March were tricky months for many reasons. My appetite began to return – a desire not just for food but for a life I couldn't yet picture, which sounds like a promising development but, actually, that's when the frustration began to kick in, that's when things got really confusing. 'The keys are in the ignition, and the engine is revving, but the car isn't moving,' I blurted out to a couple of friends down the pub. 'When will it move?' Neither of them had any answers for me and that was a problem, too, because I was desperately seeking them. I was sick of being told to hold tight, dig deep, stand firm. I had held my breath for years. We had lived a full life and in many ways we had defied the odds, never allowing the disease to control or define us. We were happy because we were in love, but our life together was predicated on maybes and make-dos, and the compromises we were forced to make unsettled us in ways we weren't always able to acknowledge – even between us.

Without a crisis to manage, I felt strangely adrift. One of the worst things friends said to me at this time was, *Now you can do anything you want*. What a terrifying prospect for a person who had kept themselves within the limits of what was possible for so long that they had become an expert at it. Worse still, this kind of provisional, conditional living was familiar to me, I had adapted to it. You may as well have spun me around several times, taken off the blindfold, and pushed me onto a busy motorway at rush hour. I was being told that the world was my oyster and yet I couldn't even bring myself to throw away a pair of slippers. How do you begin to unravel that? Where do you even start? I needed guidance, but I couldn't find it in the here and now, amongst the living, which might explain why I turned up at my mother's house with questions about my late grandmother. A story I had been told as a child was beginning to resurface as I bagged up my husband's coats and jeans, and for reasons I couldn't even fathom at the time, it seemed to correlate with my own.

SIX

I don't know much about Adam Pilarz, but I know enough. I know that he was a Sub-Lieutenant in the Polish Navy. I know he was stationed on the ORP *Orkan*, an M-class destroyer, during the Second World War. I know that he was my grandmother's first and greatest love. And I know that she dreamed of him in the water on the night he drowned at sea.

I come from a long matriarchal bloodline of dreamers. My mother claims she saw me a week before I was born. She dreamed of green slopes and white buildings and a girl with tumbling dark hair; head bowed, arms raised – as if in some kind of supplication. A plea for what, exactly, she couldn't say. In the early hours of labour, my father drove my mother to a south London maternity ward, and as they looped around the car park, she was struck by the green expanse of a grassy knoll in the dawn light. The Tetris outline of St Helier Hospital's chalk-white facade rising up like the metropolitan skyline she had imagined in her sleep. *Ah*, she thought, as her contractions quickened and my father fumbled for his car keys. *This must be tied to now.*

Unlike my mother and grandmother, I don't believe in dream-state precognition, but this doesn't mean that I haven't yearned for it from time to time, a clairvoyance that might bridge the void between two worlds and two doorways. Us and them. Past and present. The living here – and the dead somewhere out there. My grandmother's extrasensory perception might just be a family folk story, but like the childhood classics I have held on to into adulthood, it still sparks my imagination in spite of my pragmatism. There is a part of me that will always be the six-year-old girl who sneaked into her grandmother's dusty wardrobe and clambered through the musty fur coats on her hands and knees, knocking on the backboard to see if she could get to Narnia.

I began knocking on that backboard again as the daffodils began to sprout in early March. An impromptu spring clean led to a small cull of my husband's books from the top ledge of our living room shelves. I teetered on a kitchen stool and reached for dusty covers, books that we had doubled up when we first moved in together (Angela Carter, Thomas Pynchon, William Faulkner – to name a few) and had never got round to separating and discounting. *Why not yours?* he'd ask. *But why not yours?* I'd reply. And so it kept repeating. I stacked tatty copies of classics like *Mrs Dalloway* and *The Sound and the Fury* on top of other books of his that I knew I would never open: 1930s crime capers, London picture books, a coffee-table-sized hardback titled *Sex Crimes of the Futcher*. This act of erasing never got easier, the guilt hadn't lessened over time, but I reasoned with myself that by taking them into a local charity shop I was breathing new life into these paperbacks, giving them the opportunity to be read again and treasured with an enthusiasm equal to that of their previous owner.

Standing amongst piles of outgoing novels and biographies, I caressed the bookshelf with my fingers and pulled out a yellowing hardback copy of Munro Leaf's *The Story of Ferdinand*, the tale of a lonely bull who would rather sit under a cork tree and smell the flowers than fight in the ring. My grandmother regularly read this book to me at bedtime, not just sounding the words but inhabiting them somehow, plucking them off the page and animating each vowel as if they had been written for us, and us alone.

If there's one thing you should know about my grandmother, it's that she had a knack for storytelling. You could say it's the family trade. Eileen ('Lulu' for short) Marson was born on 27 November 1917 in a farm cottage in Cumbria, a rural county in the north-west of England that prides itself on its deep valleys, undulating hills and wild, careening romanticism. The verdant land of the metaphysical dreamers: Wordsworth and Coleridge and my great-grandmother, Alice Maude, who in choosing love over convention gave birth to my grandmother as a free woman out of wedlock, and in doing so must have given Lulu the wilfulness to hold on tightly to the people, and the stories, she loved. Throughout my early childhood in the 1980s, my family always joked that my grandmother was a hoarder of things, a teller of tales. Only now am I beginning to understand her squirrelling and story-weaving with the help of a pertinent Joan Didion line. That over a lifetime of accumulation, perhaps the following is true: 'There is no real way to deal with everything we lose.'

I returned *Ferdinand* to the shelf and glanced over at the mantelpiece, strewn with knick-knacks and old photographs. I have a favourite picture of my grandmother as a young woman that sits next to a self-portrait of my husband and me on a Metro carriage in Paris. Her luminous cheeks face the sun; eyes closed, mouth wide, lips open. It is a smile that is as wild and free as the woman I remember. Her loose hair cascades down her back, merging into a hazy background that if you squint at, in just the right light, reveals itself to be a dappled wood in a location that will forever remain a mystery to me. It is the kind of intimate photograph that could only have been taken by a sweetheart, a man who I heard spoken of sporadically throughout my childhood but who I never met. One afternoon, in the mid-90s, a few years after my grandmother's death, I sat cross-legged on my mother's bed and watched her open a small trinket box, inside which was a naval badge, a fragment of a life that tells only half the tale of love, trauma and loss. Which is perverse when you consider things objectively – because when a life is cut short, random memorabilia is all you have.

I asked my mother to gather Adam Pilarz's things a few days after I stacked up my husband's books. I was looking for a family correlation in this strange world of things. On a brisk Saturday morning, I took the train to my parents' house, accompanied by a notepad, a pen and a Dictaphone, because I didn't want to miss anything this time, I wanted to get everything down. 'There he is, there he is, there he is,' my mother repeated as she flipped through my grandmother's album, pointing at photograph after photograph, the surface of the kitchen table in front of her strewn with naval mementos and other scraps. Two gold-striped uniform cuffs; a black and brass epaulette; a navy sash embossed with gold lettering; an oblong scrap of paper with a name, LT. A. PILARZ, and an address, 5 LANSDOWNE PLACE, PLYMOUTH, scribbled hurriedly in blue ink. This is a mosaic, my mother told me, they're just bits and pieces, but for her, growing up in the 1950s and 1960s, the ghost of Adam had always been there.

Seventy-seven years after his battleship was sunk by the German submarine U-378, here he remains: in an emerald-green double-display photo album, with one elbow propped nonchalantly against the ship's stern and a pair of binoculars around his neck. His image sits side-by-side with a portrait of my mother as a baby, a pairing one might assume is father and daughter before learning that my mother was actually born six years after Adam died. This twin picture frame sat faithfully in my grandmother's dressing table drawer, circumnavigating two marriages, until her death in 1992.

I must have counted at least twenty photographs of Adam Pilarz on my mother's kitchen table yet neither of us know how, or even when, he and my grandmother met. Thanks to Google, we know exactly how and when he died. At 07:05 hours on 8 October 1943, the ORP *Orkan* was hit by a GNAT homing torpedo, sinking it within minutes in the Barents Sea, an Arctic shelf north of Finland nicknamed 'The Devil's Dance Floor' by sailors due to its unremitting, glacial-cold waves.

My grandmother always insisted that she saw Adam in the water, and heard him speak, in the hours that preceded his death, a narrative that increasingly intrigued me as I sifted through my husband's things, rousing a strange kind of wishful-ness, a longing for a reunion that I knew would never come.

My fixation on her sixth sense emerged at a time when I felt like my imagination was letting me down. Unlike my grandmother, I didn't experience any prophetic warnings on the night my husband collapsed with his first grand mal seizure as he waited for the kettle to boil. On the night of his death, six years later, I took a taxi home from the hospice and slept dreamlessly in our bed. Since his death, I have reimagined him in my subconscious from time to time, but only enough to count on one hand, and none of them particularly memorable. For a woman who grew up gorging herself on the gothic romanticism of the Brontës, this absence feels erroneous, almost careless. A failure on the part of my psyche to reattach a severed bond.

It's been thirteen centuries since Homer mythologised the gates of horn and ivory, the two doors that divide our dreams into those that inform us and those that deceive. Sat at my mother's kitchen table, combing through my grandmother's keepsakes, I ached for self-deception, an archway that I could pass through in the dead of night that might transport me away from the piles of dusty books. Yes, I could rationally explain my grandmother's sea story, but when I looked at her radiant face in that sepia photograph, something stirred between my head and my heart. A part of me, the storyteller, was in the water with her – and she wanted to believe.

Who's to say this isn't a part of the plan, that we're not rigged up this way, predetermined to wrestle over what we want to believe and what we actually know to be true? In ancient Mesopotamia, it was believed that dreaming was a way to see into other worlds and that the soul actually left the body to visit them. In ancient Greece, sanctuaries were built, temples known as Asclepeions, that practised the ritual of temple sleep, whereby pilgrims in search of spiritual healing were thought to be cured by prophetic dreams sent by the gods. In 1899, Sigmund Freud published his *Interpretation of Dreams*, paving the way for 'the royal road to a knowledge of the unconscious activities of the mind'. In 1943, my grandmother saw her sweetheart in the icy water and heard him call out to her as she slept. In 1953, Professor Nathaniel Kleitman and his student Eugene Aserinsky discovered the existence of REM sleep, a rapid eye movement that occurs alongside vivid dreaming. In 2018, I awoke on my hands and knees searching for my dead husband under the bed sheets because, try as I might, I couldn't find him in my dreams.

There are the things we feel, the things we know and the things we wish were true. I may doubt the veracity of prophetic sleep, but I am captivated, nonetheless, by those who are convinced of its existence. I am envious of my grandmother's faith in her grief and my mother's surety in my birth; these women, these dreamers, who can see things in ways I've been unable to visualise in my own unconscious mind. I wonder whether this wanting is due, at least in part, to the overwhelming urge I feel to tether my grief to something bigger than myself, so that I can assign some kind of predetermined meaning to it, because the alternative can sometimes feel too bleak, too arbitrary.

2,200 people are diagnosed with glioblastoma multiforme every year in England, with a median survival time of only six months. To put that clinical figure into context, that's just shy of a packed-out concert at London's Royal Festival Hall. Every

117

seat has a story to tell. A dear friend of ours once said to me that he believed my husband developed a brain tumour because his mind was just too advanced for this world. I carry that story with the same tenderness that my grandmother carried hers, and who's to say one is more probable than the other?

The memories we recall and the stories we tell cannot exist in isolation. Each one interlaces with another, and sometimes that other isn't even our own. Which brings to mind the brilliance of Walt Whitman, whose poetry I found lovingly tucked behind a photograph of Adam on that Saturday afternoon, scribbled in my grandmother's swirling handwriting. In his poem 'The Sleepers', Whitman mused on our collective unconscious and the immeasurability of our night visions: 'I dream in my dream all the dreams of the other dreamers,' he riddled. 'And I become the other dreamers.'

Maybe this is the only surety we can rely on. Maybe shared stories are all we have.

I believe that my grandmother visualised what she feared would happen, and I believe that she held on to this visualisation for the rest of her life in order to remedy a painful truth – that she wasn't with Adam in the water when he died. We don't always get to witness our losses. I didn't get to attend mine. I watched my husband finally relinquish himself to the morphinic ether and stood beside his hospice bed in silence as his lungs crackled against the flow. I have replayed this scene again and again in my mind, but the outcome is always the same. When the nurse told us that we still had time, and that I should go home to rest, I followed half of her advice. My friend

Zoë was waiting for me on the pavement outside and when we strolled to the pub on the corner, we ordered a bottle of wine.

Astronomers talk about big star energy; the larger the star, the shorter the life. When a tremendous celestial body collapses under the weight of its own gravity, it fires a burst of light and matter into the universe. And yet, when I closed my eyes that evening, I may as well have been thousands of miles beneath the water, lying prostrate on the ocean floor. I saw slate, not fireworks. I felt nothing.

Sometimes, when I try to recall a particular moment from the past, it feels like I'm holding an ice cube in my hand. Time is fluid. Memories melt. Remembrances trickle through the cracks between my fingers. Others pool in my palm and I can see my own reflection as solid turns to liquid; always changing, continuously moving.

In March 2019, a month before the *Sunday Times* published an essay on grief I had written, a photographer came to my house to take some profile shots to accompany it. I'd had a restless night and it showed. Over the space of the previous week, I had experienced a cluster of dreams that followed the same storyline, dreams that finally reimagined my husband in his hospice room, but which recast myself in his place, lying in the patient bay, waiting for him to come and visit me. When he finally arrived, his lips moved but I couldn't hear him speak. It was as if I had put him on mute.

The next morning I slathered my skin with ivory concealer, painted my lips a coral red, put on a leopard print shirt, and slipped on the red boots I'd worn to the funeral. As the photographer set up her equipment in my living room, I rearranged the furniture and sat on my new crimson sofa, a replacement for the two-seater that had cushioned my husband's seizure on the night his memory failed him and his driverless body had chased me out onto the street. After an hour of careful poses, the photographer suggested we remove two picture frames on the wall behind me to declutter the shot. I carefully removed a large black and white photograph from our wedding day, and when I looked at the tongue and groove panelling behind, I spotted two faint initials, *K & P*, brushed onto the surface with recent paint, a romantic tag he must have graffitied a few years previously when we had redecorated, now ghostly hieroglyphics that etched the walls like an engraved memorial stone in a paper house.

When the photographer finally left, I looked closer at that *K & P*, tracing the letters with my index finger, trailing the faint dribbles of wet paint that were paused in time. It brought me back to his hospice room – and to a patch of weeping ice 2,000 miles away. At the same time that my husband was taking his last breaths in south-east London, two anthropologists were releasing a documentary about loss in Iceland. A glacier was melting and had been declared dead. We now refer to Okjökull in the past tense. It *was* a glacial summit, north-east of Reykjavík, perched on top of a sprawling arch of volcanic rock. It is now a tiny cluster of thawing ice to be remembered and mourned.

Not long after I turned up at my mother's house, looking for clues that might bring me closer to Adam Pilarz in the Arctic Ocean, I started Googling phrases like 'glaciological research' and 'dying glaciers'. I was looking for experts, I was searching for facts. The melting ice I read about lingered in my mind until I sat down to write this book, when I started researching again – only this time my amateur investigations were more specific. I emailed Guðfinna Aðalgeirsdóttir, professor in geophysics at the University of Iceland, after reading about a memorial that took place at the base of Okjökull during the summer of 2019 – incidentally, six days before the first anniversary of my husband's death.

In August that year, politicians, journalists, scientists and activists stood at the graveside of 'dead ice' and unveiled a plaque inscribed with a message written by the author and poet Andri Snær Magnason, titled 'A letter to the future':

'Ok is the first Icelandic glacier to lose its status as a glacier.

In the next 200 years all our glaciers are expected to follow the same path.

This monument is to acknowledge that we know what is happening and what needs to be done.

Only you know if we did it.

August 2019

415 ppm CO_2'

When Guðfinna responded to my email, we arranged a video call, and over the course of an hour she told me that 'jökull' means *glacier* and 'Ok' means *yoke*. It was named this due to its shape, its curvaceous arms that stretched across the barren, ruptured earth. She also told me that 49 more glaciers have disappeared over the last few decades in her home country, each one a devastating casualty of accelerating climate change.

Guðfinna likens glacier ice to honey. Put a jar of it in your refrigerator and it will thicken into a paste, but leave it out on a warm sideboard and it will metamorphose, become viscous, transforming under its own weight. Our memories are stored beneath its surface, she told me. In Greenland, the past has been recorded in its ice, layer upon layer of dust particles that document 130,000 years of our earth's history. In Antarctica, scientists drilled an ice core out of its eastern plateau and discovered an atmospheric record of time that takes us back 800,000 years. Similarly to the rings of a tree trunk, each layer of buried atmosphere documents an epoch of time like pages of text, which is why Guðfinna equates the death of a glacier to the burning of books. 'You are melting it away,' she told me from her home in Iceland. 'When you make it disappear, you don't have access to it anymore.'

I became fixated with dying glaciers at a time when I was struggling to engage with my internal movements, memories and dreams. There was something about these dynamic rivers of ice that drift and weep and ooze. They seemed to reveal something about my own loss – and my grandmother's, too. I identified with the brittle surface that disguises their gooey core, the liquid centre that flows beneath seemingly motionless ice and snow. I was drawn to the disappearing layers of ancient memories, compiled and compressed, melting and thawing, and to the words we have chosen subsequently to articulate our ecological grief. Words like *memory* and *mourn* and *obituary*. It gives these frozen monuments life in their death, which, in turn, rekindled some kind of hope in me, a hope in the power of stories to affect change, something I was desperately longing for as the almond trees began to bloom.

These glaciers, like the bodies we inhabit, are time capsules that carry within them a mercurial history. Their form and memories are agile, just like ours.

Water is transparent, odourless and tasteless, covering 71 per cent of our planet's surface and constituting roughly 60 per cent of our own bodies. It is within us, it is around us. We find poetry in movement and form, and, when the unimaginable occurs, many of us go looking for it in water, as I did in those wintry months, amongst the vanishing glaciers and the restless rivers and the freezing waves.

When the writer Victor Hugo's nineteen-year-old daughter drowned at sea in 1843, pulled under by the weight of her heavy skirts, his dreams pulled him under the surface, too. He sketched them with coal dust and coffee grounds. A frightening octopus with tangled tentacles, spelling out the initials of his name. His floating daughter, an underwater nymph, reaching for a shooting star.

My grandmother never sketched her dreams on paper and yet here they are now, etched into my mind: a drowning sailor and a dying glacier, layer upon layer, compiling and compressing.

I thought about them every day that I climbed the hill between my house and my local park, conscious of the breaths

I was taking, conscious of my grandmother, too. The road was steep but I could feel her willing me onwards, my muscles tightening, giving me a sense of accomplishment as they flexed and stretched. With every step forward, I was aware of my body and the ways in which the multitudes within me were working together to keep me moving, even on the days when my heart was saying *no*, that some things are irreparable, and that maybe I was irreparable, too. That the pain was too great, the loneliness too strong.

Those were the days I walked the most, my two feet pounding, with one mouth to speak the things I feared I couldn't do.

Part III

EARTH

Then spake I to the tree,
'Were ye your own desire
What is it ye would be?'

Answered the tree to me,
'I am my own desire,
I am what I would be.'

— Isaac Rosenberg,
from 'Night and Day', 1912

SEVEN

'Watch out for the trees in there!' a woman hollered as she pulled on a taut dog lead, opened up the boot of her car, and flung her battered wellies onto a trio of flattened plastic bags inside. I slammed our taxi door shut and wandered over to my friend Jon, who was already inspecting a wooden sign that read 'WELCOME' in bright white lettering, his arms folded across his chest, inspecting the threshold between concrete and grass with an inquisitive eye.

'Thanks for the warning!' I shouted back, waving my hand in a semi-awkward salute.

'They have a life of their own today,' she continued to brief us, her voice a self-satisfied mix of jolly yet authoritative. 'I had to dodge out of the way of one; it nearly took my head off! And I counted at least *three* fallen trunks that must have come down overnight. They definitely weren't there last week. Did you hear the gales?'

'We're from London!' I replied, as if this somehow explained everything.

I watched her slide behind the wheel, considered the wellies I'd just seen her shake out, and looked down at my cracked converse, rebuking myself internally for my lack of appropriate footwear.

'Have fun!' she trilled over the barks of her retriever in the back seat. 'But be careful!'

The engine revved and her car sped away, leaving us alone in an empty car park, watching the treetops thrash and sway. I placed my hands on my hips and surveyed the sign that read 'BISHAM WOODS' above and 'INKYDOWN WOOD' below, scratching my head.

'Which one is it?' I asked, turning to Jon.

'I think it's both,' he replied.

As soon as we opened the gate, stillness transformed into a pandemonium of chatter and song. I took a deep breath, arched my back, and reached up into it. Nature buffs call it psithurism; the whispering, the swishing, the murmuring. The gentle rustle that the wind makes in the trees. An onomatopoeic word that if pronounced correctly – *sith-your-ism* – perfectly mimics the sound that it describes. I heard it all around me on this raucous April morning, 30 miles west of London. The elm trees contorted. Their leaves bristled. Weaving through bark and roots, brittle twigs snapped underfoot as a symposium of branches rustled above me, bending and chattering with the wind.

In ancient Greece, trees were believed to be prophetic beings. At Dodona, a sacred grove in the north-western region, Homer wrote of barefooted priests called the Selloi who slept under an oak tree, where they interpreted the rustle of the leaves as the divine voice of Zeus. These days, we may consider the idea of talking trees an absurd fairy tale that belongs within the pages of Tolkien's *The Lord of the Rings*, but as the grape hyacinth began to appear in late March, there were many days that I wandered out into the garden and sat under our silver birch to converse with its crinkling sounds. And on the days that I missed my husband most, it didn't seem inconceivable to me that the sounds that I heard were his.

On our sixth wedding anniversary, our first one apart, I arranged to meet Jon at Paddington station and we bought two train tickets to Maidenhead. I wanted to see the bluebells, I needed to hear the trees. I refused to feel sad. Bisham Woods is an ancient forest that rises up from the River Thames. It is said to be the original wild wood that an impulsive mole got lost in, wandering so deep into the dense thicket that he saw sharp faces in the bark, and fearing their darting eyes, hid within the dark hollow of an old beech tree.

My husband's childhood copy of *The Wind in the Willows* still sits on my bookshelf. If you flick to its opening pages, you'll find a bookplate neatly attached with his name painstakingly autographed in black ink with curling flourishes adorning the first and last letters. Another portal to an ancient grove. Its author Kenneth Grahame once wrote that his tale of adventure was written for those 'who keep the spirit of youth alive in them; of life, sunshine, running water, woodlands, dusty roads, winter firesides.'

As I stood amongst the ash and elm, I thought about the young boy who must have ambled through these majestic pillars over a century before me, looking for sprightly stories that might whisk him away from the reality at home. Grief brought five-year-old Grahame to Bisham Woods, too. When his mother, Bessie, died of a postpartum infection in 1864, his father turned to alcohol, and Grahame – along with his three siblings – were sent to live with their grandmother in a dilapidated house called The Mount in neighbouring Cookham Dean.

I wonder whether Grahame escaped to the woods to think about death, or whether he ventured through the trees to deny it altogether and invent a better world where badgers talk and mothers live. We all have them. Better worlds. In mine, my husband walks alongside me on this forest trail, and my hands are holding two children either side. One is three years old, and the other is eighteen months. I sometimes try to imagine what they might have looked like. Brown eyes are more dominant than blue, I think to myself, so they probably would have had his, not mine. Their hair, however, matches my own, deep tones that turn chestnut in the sun, along with dark freckles that are sprinkled on cheekbones and clavicles.

The eldest child I'm imagining didn't even attach and implant. We didn't get that far. The doctor graded our embryo a four on a scale of one to four – with one being the best – so I'm not sure if it even counts or whether that malformed blastocyst exists in some kind of alternative form. A ghost of a chance. A flutter of what could have been. Fluid and cells in the place of flesh and bone. We had two near-misses over the course of our marriage. One was fought for with follicle-stimulating hormones, progesterone pessaries and intracytoplasmic sperm injections. The other came by surprise, quite naturally, a few years later: two blue lines on a plastic pregnancy stick a month after we were told that my husband would have to be treated with further chemotherapy. Which sounds like a miraculous turn of events, but the pregnancy only lasted ten weeks. We don't always get to live in our better worlds; sometimes they simply dissolve, they stop multiplying, they cease to duplicate and divide, without explanation or cause.

Which is probably what brought me to this wild and untamed wood on this peculiar wedding anniversary. I could lose myself here. Looking up at the wavering trees, I felt their restlessness and it seemed to validate my own: sustained physical aches that, eight months after the event itself, still seemed to shadow my grief. I felt worn and tired – not just metaphorically but physically; tangible symptoms that panged and pulled and pulsed. Every morning I woke up with back pain and throbbing legs in addition to the break in my heart, and this may sound strange, but the heartbreak was more manageable. I had a language for it. The physical manifestations, however, seemed to run on a different kind of energy altogether.

Emotional pain peaks and troughs, but the inflammatory pain that I experienced was different. It lacked the drama we tend to associate with grief – the stabs, the lurches; the plunging, piercing and punching. Chronic pain is subdued. It likes to take its time. Some days it would dart around like a malfunctioning switchboard, but mostly it dragged itself, sluggish and slow, without much pizzazz at all. And yet it was always there, in some form or another, running in the background day after day. Pins and needles, muscles twitches, temporary numbness. Pointless and innocuous symptoms that were alerting me to the one harrowing thing I was trying to forget. I wasn't just grieving for the man I had lost, I was grieving for the body I had been left with, and in the absence of a vocabulary to articulate this, I retreated further into myself – a quiet withdrawal when all the windows were rattling.

I convinced myself that I had multiple sclerosis. A quick Google search was all it took to persuade me that my body was next and that a lifetime brain condition was now my fate, too. I scrolled through a list of early signs and ticked off symptoms that correlated with my own. Dizziness, check; fatigue, check; numbness and tingling, check; muscle spasms and weakness, check. I sat in my GP's office and babbled incoherently as she listened in silence.

'I don't want to diminish what you're telling me,' she said quietly. 'But you've been through a significant trauma and I think what you're describing is grief.'

Virginia Woolf called it a poverty of language. 'English, which can express the thoughts of Hamlet and the tragedy of Lear, has no words for the shiver and the headache,' she wrote. 'It has all grown one way. The merest schoolgirl, when she falls in love, has Shakespeare or Keats to speak her mind for her; but let a sufferer try to describe a pain in his head to a doctor and language at once runs dry.'

These words have been underlined in my copy of Woolf's essay, 'On Being Ill', but the frail pencil lines aren't mine. I suspect that my husband was planning on using this quote in his own unpublished work, and I imagine that it spoke to him quite acutely in his hospice bed about his own struggle to articulate his illness, and his body, in a way that conveyed its true meaning. My biro lines now underscore the same passage of Woolf's essay for similar reasons.

Woolf was 42 years old when she wrote about the 'ancient and obdurate oaks' that 'are uprooted in us by the act of sickness' – convalescing in bed after experiencing a breakdown that left her body with the physical imprints of its passing. Which, in a widow's world, isn't so far removed from the furrows of her grief. My husband and I overlapped here, on this page, for a reason. We were drawn to the same metaphors because grief is a kind of illness. Depression is, too. As Woolf describes, the body isn't a clear sheet of glass that the soul gazes through 'straight and clear'. And the 'creature within' cannot separate itself from the fleshy casing it inhabits like a knife. To deny this symbiosis is to reject the complexities of the body and the comparative relationship it has with the mind.

When you become chief witness to a body in slow decline, your own becomes collateral damage. I wouldn't have been able to say these words at the time. It's incredibly hard to write them, even now. I wonder how many other carers reading this have also lugged this thought around without speaking it out loud, for fear of somehow dishonouring the person that they love. A few months after my husband died, I went to my dentist, and when the hygienist casually remarked that I hadn't been looking after myself as she clawed away the plaque, I burst into tears because her words scraped too close to the bone. I hadn't been to the dentist in three years. It had been an equal amount of time since my eyesight had been tested. I couldn't remember when I'd last had a haircut. As the years go by, you lose track of yourself without even realising it.

I returned to Elisabeth Kübler-Ross' book in the spring of 2019, despite my reservations, piqued by a particular term. Anticipatory grief is the feeling of impending loss that occurs before a death and therefore has more in common with fear than with the traditional hallmarks of bereavement. In the words of Kübler-Ross, it is the uncertainty of 'going nowhere or going nowhere slowly without knowing if there will be a loss'. There is an aerodynamic drag to living like this. Imagine a skydiving free fall before the parachute has been deployed, when gravity and air resistance tussle for dominance, and the body spirals and spins. When both of these force fields are in motion, everything else becomes subsidiary to their push and pull, which is when the adrenaline really kicks in and time dissolves. Flesh billows and muscles tighten. Everything becomes squished into this one moment – a rush of *now*. You can convince yourself of almost anything at a certain altitude, with a particular weightlessness, when the adrenal glands set to work and your blood starts pumping, your eyes wholly aware of the closing distance between your body and the ground beneath you.

My anticipatory griefs were mobile, too; they moved underneath my skin. I learned to live with them, the voices within me, but I rarely spoke them out loud. I was reluctant to give them any credence. My husband would often joke about what we might be like in old age. He once imagined us sitting side by side on a coastal bench eating fish and chips, and I laughed along and engaged with his flash-forward scene whilst simultaneously harbouring a deep shame within me, the shame of knowing that we would never know each other in our seventies because our time together was more finite than that. Where do you put that shame – where does it go? I funnelled it back into my body and I tried to create someone who might outlive us both.

I was aware of the odds and I knew that they were stacked against us, but, if anything, this realisation only made me more determined to agitate the ratio. When my husband and I got married in 2013, I suspected that we may have problems conceiving but it didn't stop my overwhelming urge to start a family in spite of such fears, and I genuinely believed that we could achieve it through sheer determination like we had with everything else. We started trying on our honeymoon in Italy, hundreds of feet above the Amalfi coastline in Ravello, nine months after his brain surgery, and a year before subsequent radiotherapy and chemotherapy treatments would prevent us from continuing to try naturally.

The spontaneous afternoon frolics were soon replaced by a more methodical approach upon our return to London, as weeks turned into months, and months turned into a year. I downloaded fertility apps and I plotted my ovulation peaks with highlighter pens. I lay on a treatment table once a fortnight, mimicking yoga breaths as a pensive acupuncturist stippled my skin with needles. I cut out wheat from my diet and I held back on the weekend beers. And all the while, I blocked out the glaring obstacle that was really standing in our way: the dividing cells – not in my pear-shaped organ, but in his brain. Sometimes when he was sitting in his carver chair eating a bowl of cereal, I'd run my hand through his hair and stroke the side of my fingers over the pinky-white path of exposed scalp that tracked the surgical fault line from the back of his right ear to the top of his head. I imagined my palm as a magical suction pad and I visualised the star-shaped glial cells vibrating underneath his cranium, mobilised by the warmth of my hand, dispersing and dissolving with the sheer might of my imagination.

As the seasons rotated, windows of opportunity seemed to brick up, one after the other. Every month, a new grief arrived, meticulously on time, a messy smear of blood in my gusset that I wiped away with folded toilet paper. An ache, a sweep and a flush. And yet, we still kept trying. Even now, I'm not sure if my many attempts to conceive were a way of inventing a better world or whether it was more despairing than that. I wonder whether my dogged determination was wholly blinkered, or whether it was a disguised way to think about death in anticipation of what I knew I would eventually lose. Which sounds incredibly morbid, but it's the only way I can begin to understand the ferocity with which I rammed my body, like a square peg into a round hole, in order to make a new life.

No woman expects to find themselves splayed out in an operating room with a lubricated ultrasound probe and an egg-retrieval needle passed through their vagina, especially at the age of 32, but after two years of failed attempts I was frustrated, and angry, and cognisant of time running out. Only, it wasn't my biological clock, it was my husband's. We had recently been told that the radiotherapy had failed to slow down his tumour in the ways we had hoped. His consultant had been clipped and evasive, but the paper fact sheets we were handed as reading material weren't. Take the unquantifiable drug trialling out of the equation and he had less than a year left to live. We sat on the edge of our bed that afternoon, saying very little, because what could we say other than the obvious. He didn't want to die, and I couldn't imagine living if he did. In spite of this diagnosis – or, perhaps, because of it – we pressed on with our family plan because trying wasn't a choice, it was what we did. On a sunny morning in June, we got on a bus to King's College Hospital, the setting of so many dashes to A&E, and arrived at the Assisted Conception Unit, hidden at the back of the main building between a couple of shipping containers and a delivery loading bay.

'Is this it?' I asked my husband as we both stared at what appeared to be a semi-permanent Portakabin.

'I guess so,' he shrugged.

Neither of us took our decision to try in vitro fertilisation lightly. We both discussed the selfishness of such an act. Was it unfair to bring a baby into the world knowing what we did? Did I really want to put myself through single motherhood when it was a choice not an inevitability? Could we genuinely cope with a growing bump and an advancing tumour in tandem? My husband kept asking me these questions, I kept asking myself these questions. We sat on a park bench and when he told me that this family would be mine, not ours, that he wouldn't live long enough to be a father and to fulfil that role, I knew that he was showing me another route, not to a better world, but to an alternative life, and arguably a kinder one, only I didn't want to take it. I chose IVF, I chose hope, and I made my decision at a time when a two-day-old embryo in a petri dish was all we had to pin it on.

Every morning followed the same pattern. There was a routine to be found in the chaos. We'd get up at the crack of dawn, my husband would measure out the follicle-stimulating hormone, and I'd clumsily puncture my thigh, half-asleep, the cool liquid slinking in with a burning sting. You can lose yourself in the procedural monotony of it all, but there is a wafer-thin line between desire and dread. In 2008, neuroscientists at the University of Michigan discovered that dopamine – the hormone that we associate with motivation, arousal and pleasure – can also induce negative feelings of anxiety and fear. When I looked at the sharp tip of the needle I felt that motivational pull, but when I glanced at the worn face of the man handing it to me, the doubts crept in. How legitimate were our expectations here? How tired was too tired? I'd always considered the word *anticipation* to be a positive one, in the same way that I understood *desire* to be an affirmative emotion. But what happens when desire and dread become so inextricably confused that you start to question which is which. What happens to anticipation then?

I remember feeling jealous of all the other couples that I observed in the waiting room of the Assisted Conception Unit. 'Imagine the luxury of only having one problem to solve,' I joked over a glass of wine with my friend. I closely followed the way that they interacted with each other, pretending to read a fertility brochure when what I was really interested in was the gentle concern that pitter-pattered between them, and the awkwardness with which they engaged in this new, medicalised environment. I tried to manufacture a similar greenness but when I looked at the tote bags either side of our feet, it was impossible to follow through with the pretence. We were both so used to this – the endless waiting, the hours lost in stuffy, sanitised rooms – that we had got into the habit of packing survival kits to pass the time. When the paramedic wheeled my postictal husband out of our kitchen and onto the road outside, which happened frequently, I would do a quick sweep of the flat, grabbing my iPhone charger, a handful of magazines, a few snacks, a bottle of water and a print-out of all the medications he was taking.

> KEPPRA (LEVETIRACETAM), 125 MG, TWICE DAILY
> LAMICTAL, 175 MG, DAILY
> FRISIUM (CLOBAZAM), 20 MG IN EVENT OF SEIZURE

One night, after a particularly harrowing seizure, my husband asked if he could go back inside to fetch his book, which he proceeded to skim-read in the ambulance, the paramedics looking perplexed, as we drove to the emergency department. We were seasoned pros, we knew the drill, but I didn't want to bring that familiarity into this specific waiting room. I didn't want IVF to be just another procedure, despite knowing, deep down, that it had to be, because when you embark on IVF and chemotherapy in the same month, it *is* just another procedure. At the point when invasive fertility treatment becomes an adjunct to everything else, you pine for naivety.

When the fertility doctor motioned to a grainy splodge on the video wall a few months later, our fertilised egg ready for transfer, I knew that even if this blastocyst took, the probability that my husband would survive my pregnancy to witness the birth was slim to none. Over the months that preceded the transfer, I took this knowledge and I shoved it down, I forced it deep inside, hiding it away like the sharps box for used hormone needles that I wedged in the airing cupboard when friends came over for dinner. I had become quite numb to the realities of medical procedures because they had become such a regular component to our lives. Scientific intervention became the norm. Something goes wrong and you sit in a specialist's office with a notepad and pen, and wait for a calm, objective voice to counsel and advise. You defer to the white coats in their pristine laboratories with a blind hope that they will be able to fix things – shrink the tumour, freeze his sperm, harvest my eggs.

In 2013, eighteen months before we embarked on our IVF cycle, I stood in a cramped treatment room at University College Hospital and watched my husband being strapped to a bed whilst technicians moulded a thermoplastic radiotherapy mask to his head and neck like a dystopian scene from *A Clockwork Orange*. Two months before he died, my husband Instagrammed his chemotherapy catheter with a caption that read:

'Currently being pumped full of liquid platinum. All I
need is an evil nemesis and a plucky sidekick for this to
be my superhero origin story #platinumman #bored.'

His friends were quick to respond to this post – from 'Sending love and capes' to 'Oh, you truly are already superhuman.' The Scarlet Pimpernel approach suited him. Chivalrous aristocrat by day, daring swordsman by night. A caped crusader in his thermoplastic mask. I remember interviewing Sana Amanat, Director of Content at Marvel Comics, in 2016, for an article about her industry's patriarchal reputation, and when I asked her why the superhero narrative is so powerful she told me that it's because it's aspirational. It is designed to make us believe in the possibilities of our own human experience. Gilgamesh slaying the bull of heaven. Perseus beheading the Gorgon Medusa. Platinum Man, defying the odds with only 68 days left to live. Only the reality isn't a filtered photograph that you can caption with a witty aside. On the morning that my husband posted a catheter selfie, his 'plucky sidekick' was sitting next to him, tired and drained, reading a different kind of fairy story that she'd shoved into her tote bag. In Angela Carter's 'The Tiger's Bride', the hero is a young woman who fears her own wildness in a house full of masks. 'I was unaccustomed to nakedness,' I read as the chemotherapy trolley dribbled and beeped. 'I was so unused to my own skin that to take off my clothes involved a kind of flaying.'

I can't tell you when it happened exactly, but somewhere between the follicle-stimulating hormones and the carboplatin chemotherapy, I became so untethered from my surroundings that my body stopped desiring the very things it had actively pursued for so long. I no longer knew what I wanted, I could only tell you what I feared – an uprooting that left me numbly going through the motions without an anchorage to support me as I did so, a strange displacement, and one that made me feel increasingly distant from the things I was doing. I had pricked my thighs every morning with a detached eye, watching them swell and bruise. I had spread myself on gynaecological couches and watched clinicians plot my ovarian follicles on performance graphs. I had counted, 1-2-3, as a consultant catapulted a four-cell embryo into my uterus with a small puff of air. And I had tolerated it all – the jabs, the speculums, the pills – without feeling very much at all, other than the physicality of what I was doing, as if I had peeled away from myself completely, a rift between my body and brain that rendered me both doer and watcher, insider and outsider, participant and spectator.

This contradiction actually helped me when the IVF failed, the cramps sharpened and I saw the familiar smudge of blood when I rolled down my jeans. I placed my fingers between my thighs. There it was. A dab of maroon that smelled like copper coins. I rubbed it between my fingertips and streaked the evidence across my hand, watching it dry into a sticky, ochre trail.

After three months of intrusive procedures, my body was still saying *no*. When we first started trying to conceive, this *no* after *no,* month after month, felt like a crushing failure, but at this particular point I was so drained that I couldn't even muster the energy to grieve, and in any case, there was no space for it – not in this flat, not in this bathroom, not in this heart. With hindsight, I think there is something to be said for my uterus' refusal to acquiesce. Sometimes I even feel thankful for it. As if my body somehow safeguarded itself against further demands and constraints, a life it knew I had very little reserves to handle.

Nature has its own plan sometimes and you can't always bend it to your will, but that doesn't make the act of trying a futile one. It doesn't make the outcome a fixed tragedy, either – my childlessness is more complicated than that. On any given day, it is both a sadness and a comfort. I don't expect everyone to understand this polarity; it's taken me some time to make sense of it myself, but after years of pushing and prodding, there is some solace to be found in the spaces between these two seemingly contradictory feelings.

Things aren't always connected in ways that we can see or even fully understand at the time. I found this to be a comforting thought as I meandered over grass and earth in the spring of 2019, threading through trees that moved in a rhythm all of their own, joined together beneath the ground. I recently read that underneath every woodland is a complex trellis of roots, a subterranean network of mycorrhizal fungi that links trees and plants together in a kind of cyber structure that ecologists call the Wood Wide Web. When I took Jon's hand that April morning, I felt something new. The beginnings of empathy with myself – an emotional shift that would help me make peace with my past. Out of all the multiple paths that could have brought me here, this was the one I was on, this was the one that I had taken, and although my legs were tired, they weren't ready to give up on the rest of me – at least, not just yet.

I was meant to bring my husband to Bisham Woods, but we ran out of time. I gifted him two conifer trees in this 86-hectare forest for our fifth wedding anniversary, four months before he died. 'Somewhere to call our own,' I wrote in the accompanying card. Two saplings in an ocean of green that I had no chance of ever locating but that I still felt connected to as I walked ahead with thoughts of the four of us, two people and two embryos, entwined through the soil, blood seen, and blood lost.

Our story didn't end with IVF. I found out I was pregnant about a year after our failed cycle. A last gasp – and an unexpected one. We were stunned, we were thrilled. Butterfly flutters soon developed into morning sickness and food aversions – a promising sign, I was told. We even started discussing baby names, with my husband taking typeface fonts as his inspirational cue.

'How about Helvetica if it's a girl, or Dingbats if it's a boy?' he joked.

A few weeks later, I sat and stared at my dinner, pushing spirals of stodgy pasta around the plate. I had often wondered what this unfurling would feel like, but now it was finally happening, it unsettled me in ways I wasn't prepared for. The belches and hiccups dislodged me. The smell of tea leaves made me gag. My head throbbed as I tried to write. I waded through swampy puddles on my way to work. Everything felt so *slow* and so *heavy* and so *off*. After years of failed attempts, my body had finally given in to my demands – so why didn't it feel right? Shouldn't a wanted pregnancy be enjoyed not disliked? The reality is that my pregnancy was a paradoxical one. Yes, it gave us hope, but it also created another depleted body, and that scared me. Even now, I swing between two versions of myself: the woman who was thrilled to be pregnant, and her doppelganger: the woman who was afraid of what that really meant for her when death was so near. With time to familiarise myself with the changes in my body, I'm sure that this fear would have lessened over time, becoming quieter, more nuanced – who knows? I can only speculate because ten weeks was all we had.

When I began to spot and my GP suggested an early scan, I persuaded my husband to rest at home whilst I sat alone in another waiting room – this time in an early pregnancy unit – clutching a numbered ticket in my right hand. The plastic seating niggled my back, causing me to fidget from left to right. As I scanned the room, my eyes paused on a man in a suit aggressively typing on a laptop that teetered on his knees. I glanced at his partner sitting next to him, recognising the glazed look in her bloodshot eyes, the detached gaze, the middle-distance stare that said, *I'm not here.*

It would take doctors a further two weeks to confirm what I already knew. I stared numbly at the empty black ellipse on the ultrasound screen, a sixteen-millimetre gestational sac with nothing inside, and when the plastic wand was finally removed, a nurse handed me a paper towel to wipe away the sticky trails of gel between my thighs. I had become familiar with the protocol. I had opened my legs in countless examination rooms over the years, and this February morning was no different, only it was the closest we had come to realising a family, and today was Valentine's Day, and the absurdity of this realisation churned inside me as I pulled up my knickers between the curtains.

A few hours after I was handed an unstapled miscarriage leaflet on a noisy NHS ward, I sat in a cinema seat at the British Film Institute watching Gene Kelly tap and Charleston to the jaunty melody of 'I Got Rhythm'. My husband stroked my hand. In times of trauma, this is what we did, we diverted ourselves from the reality. Some people anthropomorphise woodland animals to escape grief, and others immerse themselves in George Gershwin scores. Distraction is a tool, but it's rarely a fix.

Every morning that I arrived at the hospital where my husband was dying, I walked past the day surgery unit where my placenta and empty gestational sac were suctioned away. Some anembryonic pregnancies take care of themselves, but mine needed a helping hand. I numbly read over the paperwork as clinical words jumped out at me such as 'evacuation', 'surgical management', 'non-viable' and 'pregnancy tissue'. I was told that the surgeon would dilate my cervix before my 'retained products of conception' would be removed. I was informed that these 'products' would be sent to a lab for testing. I gave permission for them to be, later, cremated. I circled the 'YES' for a blood transfusion in case of excessive bleeding and I signed on the dotted line.

A few hours later, I woke up in the recovery bay with a sanitary pad between my legs and a cup of sweet tea on my bedside table. I noticed a few faint cramps, but the feeling, that feeling, was gone. How can you grieve for something that was never really there? I didn't have the answers then, nor did I on that Saturday in April as Jon and I strolled hand in hand through the bluebells, but maybe I didn't need them anymore. I had begun looking for something else.

The leaves began to susurrate again, louder this time, and as we walked out into the car park, they sounded like breaking waves.

EIGHT

I shaped three of my fingers into a fleshy prism and placed them underneath my dress. A soft caress across my stomach, a skim of the waist, a few teasing loops around my belly button, and then down to the nub of the matter. I encircled it at first, tracing its creases – to get my bearings, and feel its plump form – before splitting my index and middle fingers into a scissors-like formation, pressing firmly either side of the soft, pinky folds, *up and down, up and down*, with a sliding motion that tickled at first, then shivered, then throbbed. I took my time, giving myself a midway pause to really enjoy what I was doing, one hand brushing through the waxy hair that scattered and spread like a black cloud of curls between my legs.

It had taken me decades to finally accept myself, to be able to look at my body in its natural state without feeling that I ought to modify it in some way. I remember spotting my first protruding hairs when I was a child with a shameful panic that I carried with me into adolescence and beyond into adulthood. They looked ugly to me: these coarse, dark wires breaking through the surface like spidery legs. I was used to smoothness, not these thick antennae, and something about them seemed invasive to me as I stared downwards, my perspective skewed into a funnel-like beam.

I yanked two of them out with a pair of tweezers that I found in my parents' bathroom cabinet. I was only ten at the time. Women are taught to groom ourselves with blades and creams and pots of molten wax, and we are schooled to do it from such a young age that it is almost impossible to extricate ourselves, and our desires, from the wants and the gaze of others. *This is mine*, I thought, as I recalled that ten-year-old girl, and looked down at the untamed bramble between my legs, handling it tenderly, widening my hand and combing through swirls of hair with my fingertips, before brushing the back of my palm between the soft, inner contours of my thighs. The touch of my skin brought me back to myself and I drew her upwards again, rubbing the back of my thumb over the pea-shaped gland I had ignored for so long.

It is estimated that every clitoris has around 8,000 sensory nerve endings, and yet for the last two years, I hadn't been able to feel a single one, as if an electrical cable had been cut and the current had nowhere to go. The worst part was that this severance had gone largely unnoticed. There was no space in my head to acknowledge the creeping numbness, and no way of reversing it anyway. I imagine that it must have occurred in the midst of my fertility treatment, but I have no way of pinpointing an exact dash on the timeline that says *here*, this is when it happened, this is when I stopped feeling.

I hadn't had sex since my miscarriage. We had tried, we attempted it time and time again, but nature is cruel, and the physicality of the illness took over any desire we both still had. Add years of programmed baby-making into the equation and I had genuinely forgotten what they were there for – those 8,000 nerve endings – and where I wanted them to go, what I wanted them to do; so they went nowhere, and did nothing, dissipating into the rest of me with such efficiency that I didn't even have time to consider what this osmosis really meant.

The first time I felt them again was a Sunday afternoon, whilst I was reading a magazine on the sofa. Somewhere around my thirty-sixth birthday, the threadlike roots began to course and current again, extending from the inside of my thighs to the outside curve of my waist and downwards again into the earth of knees and ankles and toes. Over the coming weeks, the urges became more frequent and more intense, spreading wider and deeper. I went back again and again, and each time felt more freeing than the last. I wanted more of it. After years of detachment, something was rewiring and it was so instinctive that it required little effort and even less analysis – which was a new one for me. I overthink everything. I'm the kind of person who can keep herself awake at night with the realisation that she has nothing specifically to worry about. It's the same kind of insomnia that occurs when I'm in a tranquil holiday spot, away from London's ambulance sirens and aeroplane drones, and in the absence of any noise around me, the sound of this silence keeps me awake, making me toss and turn in the same way that my neighbour's burbling television can back home.

'It feels different,' I told my friend Zoë.

'How exactly?' she asked.

'I don't know,' I replied.

I did and I didn't. I knew something revolutionary was happening, but it felt so pure and unbridled that words seemed to let it down, they didn't seem to do it justice. I wasn't sure how to explain the miraculousness of this feeling without sounding like a hysterical teenager who'd just discovered where everything was for the first time and couldn't shut up about it. But that's essentially what it was: a blossoming discovery in the dark, the arrival of multiple sensations that felt entirely new to me, colouring outside the lines, layering up, intensifying and expanding. Waves of pleasure, not grief, although how strange that both can ripple and undulate with a similar rhythm. Over the coming months, I became more adventurous, experimenting in ways that tested these new connections and pushed the boundaries – not only in terms of what had pleasured me before, but what could pleasure me now. *What next? How about this?* I chopped and changed my positions. Standing up, knees to chest, legs pointed down, left ankle raised up, two heels on the wall. I explored myself like never before: across the sofa, on the floor, in my bed – a piece of furniture I was yet to fully repossess and reclaim.

I still slept on my side of the bed. There seemed to be an invisible line that perforated it in half, and for some reason lying across it felt as intrepid as crossing a border into an unknown land. A few weeks before my husband was rushed into hospital with a suspected stroke, we stood on the fifth floor of Peter Jones in West London and picked out a new mattress and a pair of pillows. Two unsuspecting shoppers who had no way of knowing that such purchases would turn out to be so needless. He only got to sleep on that pillow a couple of times. Sometimes, in the middle of the night, I'd glance over at it, and its newness seemed to goad me in the dark; a plump swathe of unblemished cotton without a faceprint to dent it out of shape. I didn't even like to stick my right elbow out, lest I traverse into a space where I didn't belong.

Technically speaking, that mattress was mine for the taking, I was free to spread out in whichever configuration I chose – vertically, horizontally, diagonally, even – but in reality, my body felt hampered by my head, so it remained habitually on the left-hand side. To occupy that expanse to the right of me would be to appropriate it, in the same way that I annexed a second shelf for myself in the bathroom, swapping his shaving cream and deodorant for my face primer and cleansing fluid; only the bed seemed to be a different frontier altogether, a step too far, perhaps. There was something about laying my head in the exact spot where his used to dream that felt wrong – cold-hearted, even. I wasn't sure how to take up such an intimate pocket of space in my own home without feeling like I was encroaching on the past, a territory that wasn't mine.

Each framework tells a different story, but when life splinters, some narratives overlap. When the author Deborah Levy divorced at the age of 50, she also struggled with which part of the mattress to use and so she alternated between the head and the foot, placing a pillow on either end depending on her particular mood. Sometimes she faced north, other times she headed south. Over time, she put two pillows at either end. 'Perhaps this was a physical expression of being a divided self,' she wrote in *The Cost of Living*, 'of not thinking straight, of being in two minds about something.' Or perhaps it was a self in flux – not a binary separation, but a fluidity of movement, intermixing and mingling.

Death and divorce. They aren't always so far apart. When I began exploring my body again, I made a deliberate decision to traverse my mattress, too. Not every day, but on occasions where I felt confident enough to do both. I would place my head on his pillow, allowing the weight of my skull to sink down into it and make its mark as my fingers wended their way downwards looking for a climactic peak to catapult me upwards and away. *It is time to make new memories here*, I thought to myself – not to replace the old ones, but to loosen me enough from them so I could start feeling something else again.

When I was dating in my early twenties, the bed was a place to hide, and intimacy was a destructive pursuit I wilfully lost myself in, submitting to crude men who mistook roughness and blunt enthusiasm for passion. They never really took the time to ask what made me feel good, so I never really discovered what did. I put up hurdles. I withheld the things I knew they wanted. I denied my own urges. There was no nourishment to be found in those bedrooms because it was always a performance of sorts and I never felt truly comfortable in my own skin. Most of the time I didn't even regard these men highly enough to explain my contradictory behaviour to them, the manner in which I would very publicly pull them in before privately pushing them away.

The bed isn't always an exciting prospect when it can also double up as a stage. I didn't really understand this when I was younger, but grief has a knack of exposing all your past losses and shedding new light on them. The bed can do that, too. It sits at the epicentre of things, witnessing our languor, our titillations and our adventures. It's where many of us are conceived, it's where some of us are born, it's where our relationships play out – and, as I painfully observed in my husband's hospice room, it's often where we die. The bed can stretch out beneath us like an infinite archipelago of encounters waiting to transport us, yet it can also be a place of solitude and isolation, a state of regret and self-doubt. There are those who resist between headboard and foot, just as there are those who submit. In a world that demands so much of us, there are many more who hide and conceal.

I didn't really know what an equal partnership physically felt like until I met my husband and my defences came down. I told him all the things I had buried for so long and, as he listened quietly, lying next to me, I finally realised how beautiful silence can be when you've been running away from it for so long. You might assume that, given this history, my sofa explorations would have involved my late husband – at least a little, surely occasionally – but in reality, my imagination had other ideas. Perhaps this was a way of separating myself from my grief, but I'm more inclined to think that it was a way of asserting my desires in accordance with myself – arguably for the first time – irrespective of any man, including my husband. Was this a common reaction? I genuinely asked myself this question. On a weekday night, I opened my laptop and began searching for narratives that matched my own but I struggled to find them. About an hour later, I came across a *New York Times* article titled, 'When a Partner Dies, Grieving the Loss of Sex', and clicked on the link.

Sexual bereavement wasn't a term I was familiar with and it piqued my interest. When Dr Alice Radosh's husband of 40 years died in 2013, she was perfectly capable of handling the finances and the car and the household repairs, but what she really struggled with was the loss of sexual intimacy after decades of physicality with her long-term partner. In the absence of any literature that spoke to her about this kind of grief, she did what any researcher would do in her predicament: she decided to author her own. Radosh, a research psychologist with a doctorate in neuropsychology, co-authored a paper published in 2016 titled 'Acknowledging Sexual Bereavement: A Path out of Disenfranchised Grief'. Surveying 104 women aged 55 and over, Radosh found that 72 per cent anticipated that they would miss sex with their partner when they died, 67 per cent imagined they'd want to talk about it, and yet 57 per cent said it would not occur to them to initiate a conversation with a widowed friend, findings that led Radosh to conclude that:

'A culture of silence surrounds feelings of sexual bereavement following a partner's death and these feeling [*sic*] are left unvalidated. In silence they become disenfranchised grief – a grief that is not openly acknowledged, socially sanctioned and publicly shared.'

How strange to identify with a term that is based on an experience so different from your own. We tend to think of widowhood in terms of an older demographic because the average age of a widow(er) *is* older. According to the Office for National Statistics, the median age for becoming a widow(er) in 2017 was 76. There was a 41-year age gap between me and the majority, and I felt it acutely as I read Radosh's research paper, desperate to find narratives that even remotely correlated with my own, even if this meant that I was trying to identify with a group of widows who were old enough to be my mother, and in some cases, grandmother. Unsurprisingly, this pulled me into a conflicted no man's land. Whilst my reignited libido did feel related to the sexual bereavement Radosh had written about, it seemed to be going off on an entirely different tangent, fuelled by a lust for sweaty physicality as opposed to anything sentimental. I didn't appear to be missing the sex I had with my husband, I found myself being drawn in the opposite direction, a different kind of disenfranchised grief that left me feeling roused and confused.

My eyes darted around packed tube carriages at rush hour, sweeping for body parts. Arms, in particular, got my attention. Muscular biceps, sturdy forearms, broad shoulders, expressive hands. I'd size them up and estimate their capabilities. *That guy would be able to pick me up*, I'd say to myself. *That one would feel quite weighty if he pinned me down.* A flash of animalism followed by a low lying rustle of guilt. *Could he hear me?* I wondered. Not the man in the shirt and tie, leaning against the handrail on the Jubilee Line, but the spirit of the man I had married – the husband in my heart.

This fetishisation was an offshoot of my grief, but it was also the result of watching a relentless disease wreak havoc on my husband's body – and my own. Throughout the years that we tried to conceive, I'd often spy families out and about in our neighbourhood and closely observe the gurgling babies in their prams as I queued for my takeaway coffee. In the last year of our life together, this observational preoccupation shifted into something that I shamefully kept to myself for fear of what it said about me and what I valued in others. I would pick out athletic-looking couples and peruse their bodies, surveying their honed anatomy with a roving eye. One morning, I watched a man and woman chatting nonsense in their workout gear as I chomped on a bacon sandwich in my local cafe, and I felt covetous of what I saw across the room, which wasn't an envy aroused by any particular possession or quality that they had, I was simply jealous of the bodies they inhabited, free of the stresses and strains of pills, seizures, injections and surgery.

Over the years, the body became a functional structure I needed to save and defend. I no longer cared what it looked like or how it felt, I only worried about the fundamentals, what was needed to keep it going. The breaths, inwards and outwards; the heart, expanding and contracting; the neurons, whizzing and dancing. In the final weeks of my husband's life, I watched his body shut down, component after component, like light bulbs switching off, one by one, in a skyscraper of glowing rooms. A few days before he died, I walked him to the bathroom, and when his balance faltered, his legs did, too, slamming his torso onto my back as I crumpled against the wall, pushing myself out like a life raft underneath him to try and cushion his body as he fell.

My body had become all the things it couldn't do. This was the body I had been left with. It had got to the point where I no longer liked looking at it, and I couldn't imagine anyone else wanting to, either. About a month before our wedding anniversary, the one I spent in Bisham Woods, my counsellor sat quietly as I cried in my chair. When she asked me what I saw when I looked in the mirror, I told her that my body seemed broken to me. It felt used and discarded. I felt tired and worn. *Damaged goods*, I said – and who wants that?

'I want you to go lingerie shopping,' she said.

'Is that really necessary?' I replied, as I blew my nose into a damp tissue.

'You don't have to buy anything, that's not the point of the exercise,' she carried on. 'I want you to try things on and really look at yourself in the changing room when you're doing it. What makes you feel attractive? What looks good? And I don't want you to think of a man when you ask yourself these questions.'

A week later, I was browsing through silk and lace with Zoë in a central London department store.

'This is a waste of money,' I sighed, as I held an embroidered bra up to myself before putting it back on the rail. 'Who's going to see it?'

'You are,' she replied.

That evening, I stood in front of the full-length mirror in my bedroom and asked myself what I saw. I had tried the same exercise a few hours earlier, in a plush, velvet-curtain changing room that smelled like fresh carpet and woody notes of vanilla and musk. I skimmed over my body, readjusting the tight straps that stretched over my bony shoulders and curling my thumb into the elastic of the matching briefs below. I flicked the seam with a *snap* and a *ping* against my skin. The overhead light was bright, highlighting every crease and dimple, so I squinted my eyes and turned to the side. *Try again*, I thought, but from this angle all I could see was a scaly spread of blemishes that crept from under my ears, to the nook of my neck and down the length of my back – the reddened mark of a skin condition that had been exacerbated by anxiety and stress.

This wasn't working, at least it wasn't working here, so I made a purchase and brought it home, dimming the lights and standing a little further away from my own reflection. When I looked at the figure in the glass, I set to work, making a mental list of all the body parts that had got me here. Big blue eyes that had seen it all and yet still wanted more. A plump mouth full of words. The soft incline of my neck as it curved into my shoulders – a sturdy yoke that carried the weight of my head and everything in it. A narrow waist that tapered into widened hips that liked to swish and sway down pavements. A pair of long, willowy arms to cuddle and cosset the people I love. Stout and muscular legs that take after my father, much to my chagrin, but which had carried me through the worst of it and brought me to this very spot I was standing on right now.

Not a tired body, but a capable one, I counter-proposed. This wasn't the reflection of a woman who had stood back and watched her husband die; this was the body of a woman who had stepped in to help him live – and now she was asking for the same in return.

'Why am I so good at looking after the people I love,' I asked a friend, 'and yet so terrible at taking care of myself?'

Something had to change, I had to change, *I was changing* – and I seemed to be propelled by this energy without knowing where it was going to drive me next. Take this one Thursday evening in April 2019, for instance.

'Is this the right place?' I said, turning to Jon, before looking down at the map on my phone.

We stood awkwardly in a vegan cafe, twirling around tea cups and plates of cake, before spotting a discreet curtain to the left of us draped behind a sign that read:

'Women's Erotic Emporium
Come in and have a peek!'

I brushed the curtain aside and wandered through, looking around the room of gadgets and toys, a cabinet of curiosities packed full of tactile trinkets that glimmered like jelly sweets waiting to be plucked. Bullet vibes, clitoral stimulators, g-spot bunnies, remote-control egg vibrators, air-suction massagers. This was definitely the place. About a fortnight earlier, Jon and I had been sitting in our local pub and he had talked about a shop called Good Vibrations that went by the tagline, 'Pleasure is your Birthright'. The shop was founded by a sex therapist called Joani Blank in 1977 on 22nd and Dolores Street in San Francisco, a city where Jon had lived in the nineties. As he recalled the friendly, sex-positive, woman-centred interior, we began looking for a London equivalent, finding it in East London, tucked away on an unassuming street corner in Shoreditch. I had no desire to hit a seedy emporium in Soho and navigate myself through all the paraphernalia that seemed geared towards the kind of male gaze I was trying to break away from. I needed a physical space, a tangible location where I could draw an X to mark the spot, the intersection between where I had been and where I wanted to go.

I left Jon engrossed in a paperback copy of *Sometimes She Lets Me* – a collection of 22 butch/femme erotic stories – in the library corner of the shop and sauntered around the various display tables, helpfully themed, picking up objets d'art and placing them back down again, immersed in the act of touch, feeling my way, stroking the smooth, velvety silicone that curved so pleasurably into the palm of my hand.

'Do you need any help?' a friendly shop assistant asked as I fondled an electric green leaf-shaped vibrator.

I looked across the room at Jon, who was still absorbed in his book, before looking back at her with a smile.

'I don't know what I'm looking for,' I replied – and just like that, I set myself free.

It wouldn't be long before I felt the weight of someone else again, although I had no way of knowing this at the time. My emancipation wasn't in expectation of that moment. It couldn't be a prelude to somebody else's suite. It belonged to me – and me alone.

A few weeks after my East London shopping trip, a parcel arrived, sent from my friend Cecilia in West Yorkshire. When I opened the jiffy bag, I unwrapped a framed photograph that she had taken a few months previously, near to where she lives. A wintry tree stands stoically on a hill enveloped in snow, a thick swathe of white, accentuated by a halo of green directly under its bare branches. In the accompanying card, Cecilia told me that the warmth of the tree's roots had radiated upwards, below the surface, and melted the snow on the grass above.

Some call it 'thaw circles' and when I looked at this liquefying crown, I saw the parts of myself that were yet to dissolve.

NINE

He asked me what I wanted. I replied, 'To explore some-one's body,' but what I really wanted to explore was myself. Tiny movements I could feel. A tingling kinaesthesia where previously there was none. A set of far-off coordinates that I'd as yet failed to seek out, in fear of what they might do, how they would feel, or even, perhaps, how they could hurt.

It was approaching midnight. I placed my half-drunk negroni down on the coffee table in front of me and looked around the room scanning for context. Shiny faces, flirtatious poses. Metal countertops and long-legged bar stools. A hyena squeal followed by a chorus of hollow cackles that bounced from mouth to wall to glass and back again. Random minutiae that you tend to notice when life slows down and the world condenses into fluid beads on a window pane.

I was good at doing this: squinting my eyes, observing the landscape and blocking out the rest. Every afternoon that my husband snoozed in his hospital bed, I'd traipse down endless sanitised corridors looking for a way out. Right at the lifts, left at the Costa concession stand, passing exit signs and waiting rooms, searching for fresh air, beeping traffic and a trio of signal bars on my iPhone screen. A whoosh of the doors and a gust of air. From lino to concrete and sky. I would weave through the car park, threading through ambulance vans and speeding taxis, turning right onto the main road, passing wheelchairs and IV drips and hollowed faces puffing on spindly cigarettes, headed for the park next door. Sometimes I would walk around the bandstand, other times I liked to sit under a tree. The faint drone of traffic soothed me as I would brush my fingers against grass and leaves and my eyes would follow wisps of litter that floated and twirled in the breeze.

'Someone's body,' he asked, 'or mine?'

I could hear the sound of rustling leaves as the barman rattled a cocktail shaker across the room. Words escaped me that night, or maybe they were never there to begin with, lost in a flurry of *someone's* and *yours* and *I don't know*.

I could have picked any random man in any bar, but it was this particular person in this specific hotel lounge, and I wasn't sure what that meant. All I knew was that we had courted it for months – across thousands of miles – and although we were batting across the whys and wherefores on this three-seater sofa, it was futile to pretend that there was any other path in this building other than the one that led to his room from the lift outside.

I scanned the dark recesses and observed the drunken dance moves that punctuated the bland, sapless space that we'd found ourselves in. A trimming of plush velvet seating lined the edges of the room and a splattering of identikit wall art blended into the dimmed lighting around the centralised bar. Two women bounced around, drinks in hand, as their male friends watched from their chairs. A birthday gathering was peaking to the right of us, a rabble of voices getting louder and louder, as voices tend to do when they aren't being heard. I tilted my head and turned my body towards his: an instinctive response to the loud shuffle of late-night hits that blared through a speaker above our table. The volume increased and I strained to catch his words – holding on to some, letting go of others – leaning in, looking straight, holding back. 'I don't have any answers', I said. 'I only know where I want to go.' Sometimes his eyes met mine, but mostly they darted away. Droplets of condensation trickled down the sides of my cocktail glass, pooling in a ring around its base, and I wiped it away with a serviette before leaning in again, this time brushing mouth on skin as I curled mine under his. He was both a friend and a stranger, and I needed them both that night, in this vapid bar, miles away from home, halfway between the glaciers and the thawing snow.

The first time I undressed myself for a man, he wasn't even in the room.

'Go upstairs and take your clothes off,' he said, in a manner that was half-suggestive, half an order. 'I'll be up in a minute.'

I quietly climbed the stairs of his grandmother's house and did what I thought was expected of me, only it didn't feel good, this act of unbuttoning, it made me feel ashamed. As I loosened the rivets of my jeans I could hear the kettle boiling in the kitchen downstairs, a quiet whistling that was occasionally interrupted by a slam of cupboard doors. He was making tea – he may have suggested that, too, but I don't remember. I folded my clothes in a neat pile at the foot of the bed and wondered what I was supposed to do here. Who was I supposed to be?

The room smelled musty, as if the walls had absorbed all the decades of cigarette smoke and boredom and had yellowed into a brittle, peeling crust to detain it here indefinitely. I brushed my hair and lay on top of blankets and sheets. Is this what he wanted? Is this what I wanted? *No, this is ridiculous*, I thought. I felt exposed, so I got under the duvet and closed my eyes, trying to regulate my anxious thoughts. *This is your fault*, I chastised myself internally. It was my fault for not doing it sooner like everyone else. I waited for the jingling of teaspoons on ceramic followed by a stomp of trainers on the carpet, muffled sounds, *thud thud thud*, a creak of the door, then a look that said, *Is this what you have for me?*, as he placed two mugs down on a nearby surface and casually removed his t-shirt and trousers. I was nineteen and I wanted to please. He was nineteen, too, but was already adept at recognising the value of such wilfulness in someone like me. Only there was hesitation, too, because I knew, deep down, that this wasn't good enough for me, even if I couldn't say it out loud on this suburban street, inside this stale terrace house, in a pallid town that I was desperate to escape from but didn't know how.

'This is *really* going to hurt,' he said, eyes on mine, lying on top of me – and it did, a little later, but not for that reason, not in the way that he meant.

I'd like to say that this first experience of mine was simply a passive memory, but for many years it took up residence in the back of my head, a distant recall that challenged any trust I had in the possibility of sex as an exchange, rather than a sparring contest for some kind of control over my thoughts. For many years, sex always felt that way – a power game, a way to control me, which sometimes was the case, but more often than not was due to my own mistrust. Claustrophobia can be tricky to handle. I never knew what to do with mine, which meant that any physicality that occurred became something to push away when it felt like the body pressing down on mine was crudely crushing the parts of me that I'd yet to claim for myself.

'When you stare off into the distance like that, where do you go?' my husband regularly asked. It's the same question an ex-boyfriend once posed. Absence and intimacy. How many of us are unnerved by the enclaves that we perceive others are holding back from us? I often wonder about this when I think back to my first sexual encounter. That nineteen year old chose not to sleep with me that night. Perhaps my silence unnerved him, maybe a look displeased him. Who knows, he might've heard my internal voices. Whatever the reason, it wasn't what he expected – and something quickly shifted.

'You don't trust me,' he said in a tone that bordered on irritation. His body pressed down on mine and I wondered how two people could be so close when they were that far away. I looked directly at him and said nothing as he slid off me with a world weary sigh, slumping onto the mattress before reaching over to the nightstand for a cigarette.

Love and sex. Desire and rejection. It's the dance that we do, the push and pull of two poles, and I learned it from a young age. Place a couple of magnets closely together and they will either draw together or repel apart. I thought about this in the hotel bar as I swilled my negroni and took another sip. I had a flashback to an ex-boyfriend and the last time we were in bed together. I nodded a silent consent and he turned me over, burying my face in the pillow, because he'd given up on the reality and could no longer bring himself to look at it in my eyes, a humiliation that has diffused in me over time, but will never fully dissolve. If anything, it has reshaped and reformed over the years into something so far removed from that initial distress that it can only be described as a certainty, a sureness, deep down in my body where previously there was shame.

I don't think that I'd ever really fixed myself on someone and shown them my intent before. I'd certainly never made the first move with any degree of confidence. What a time to mutate. The hotel bar shimmered and when my lips parted first, the sheer act of it thrilled me. A few months earlier a friend of mine warned me that the first time probably wouldn't be enjoyable, and I knew that logically he was right – insofar as it had been some time since I'd felt that kind of gratification, I'd been with my husband for ten years, and my moods were still yo-yoing. I had no idea how I might respond to sex as a grieving widow and I was aware of the many possible scenarios that might play out that evening. What if I burst into tears? Maybe I'd get angry and shout. I could react in the same way that I had, at the age of eleven, when I arrived at my grandfather's funeral in a packed out church and stifled a laugh as I walked down the aisle because the sheer scale of the congregation in front, the vaulted ceiling above, and the depth of my grief inside, overwhelmed me. And yet somehow I didn't think that any of these options were going to be the reality for me. At least, not with this person, not tonight, and I couldn't explain why – nor did I want to. The self-assurance was liberating. It seemed to be channelled from somewhere else entirely.

In late April, a few days after my first wedding anniversary alone, I had wandered through a Dorothea Tanning exhibition at the Tate Modern and stopped at a self-portrait that she'd painted in 1942. I was there for a while: reading, watching, looking – treading the vast perimeters of her gaze. In Tanning's own words this oil painting on canvas is 'a dream of countless doors'. Her body faces towards us, regal jacket unbuttoned, breasts uncovered. If you look closely at the bustle of her skirt you realise that it isn't made of silk or velvet or any recognisable textile, but a tangled mesh of twigs and branch-like bodies that writhe, alive and untamed, and yet her body is still, her stare is fixed outward – towards us. Look to the floor of the empty room where she stands, and her bare feet point towards a winged creature with yellow eyes, curled talons and attentive ears. Her left hand grasps the nearest doorknob, as one frame leads to another and another down an infinite corridor of open doors. Has she arrived or is she leaving? Is she alone or does someone look back at her? It's impossible to tell. 'Everything is a miracle, iridescent, obsessive and alive,' Tanning once mused on her painting. 'Everything is in motion. Also, behind the invisible door (doors), another door.'

I sat on the bed and loosened my sandal straps before sliding backwards across the covers, placing both hands either side of the mattress, a position that propped up my body into an open recline: palms down, shoulders wide, eyes up – as if to say, *Here I am. What are you waiting for? Help me feel something else.* He kneeled over my hips and I dropped my weight to take his as he pinned me onto the bed, burrowing into the nook of my neck. I'd spent months imagining this pressure, his heaviness, the solid force of someone else's body on top of mine, a carnal reminder that I was still here and that someone could still see me, iridescent and obsessive and alive. We spoke with demanding mouths and gliding fingertips. A firm hand fondled its way between my legs from the back of my knee to the incline of my thigh and I willed it upwards as it pressed and plied at an assertive pace that I happily relinquished myself to. Speed and force and movement. I desired it, I asked for it, I wanted more. Where to, what next? *Hold me here, press it there.* He tugged my hair and I felt the resistance as I pulled it back, undoing the ties of my wrap dress as if I was shedding my own skin.

A week later, my legs were wrapped around his. Eyes closed, hips pressed, mouths open. He scooped me up, lifting me from the bed, and I pushed myself downwards feeling the strength of his forearms pulling me in as I did so, my feet dangling either side. I felt the power in my abdominal muscles, too, rising and falling, filling the rest of me up with a *glug glug glug*. I tightened my knees around his waist and felt the pulses between them, upbeat followed by offbeat. I had held my body together for the last nine months and now someone else was doing the work for me, if only for a few hours, and for that brief moment I felt weightless and whole.

Let go, and let out. *Gather him in.*

I liked it when he positioned me and I enjoyed being under him the most. He got the gist, anticipating my cues and we roamed across the mattress like two nomads with no place to settle. Pin my wrists, lever that leg, press me back. I wanted him to take it, take it all: my body, the sadness, this inertia. *Do something else with it*, I thought, as we crumpled the bedding, my feet arching against his back as I rocked, to and fro, with both tension and ease. A flutter of parallel paths circled around my waist before they tingled downwards, stretching across my thighs. Imagine being strung together with gossamer thread through the very core of you, then imagine someone pinching its tip from the top of your head and pulling it upwards towards the ceiling, higher and higher, lengthening its span, extending your vertebrae. Then repeat and reverse. It spun itself gently from the lobes of my ears, shivering down the arch of my back, over and under, through tendon and muscle, before looping around my big toe in ever-tightening circles.

I felt the branching roots inside me, spreading and radiating with every swivel and twist. My body felt stretched, pressed and palpated. It was being handled, I was being enjoyed, and my insides tingled and glowed with activity. It was a feeling I'd forgotten. The buzzing and the humming. The susurration beneath the skin. Words seemed superfluous in the company of such sensations, and when they were finally spoken they punctured the air with clumsy question marks and full stops that seemed to break up these rhythms and interrupt my natural flow. *No*, I thought, *I won't do this here*. From solid to liquid and back again. I fished my underwear from the floor and lay on top of the sheets, saying nothing, fixating on the closed window in front of me, listening to the muffled sounds of traffic and pedestrians that tootled and warbled outside. I had surrendered myself to the physicality of this moment: to touch and sight and taste. The smoothness of his skin, the sweat on the sheets, the salt on my tongue. I wanted to keep going, and keep going, and keep going, but when our bodies stopped moving the walls seemed to take over: contracting, asserting their lines, reducing the space.

'I don't live here,' he said – and I replied, 'I know,' when what I really wanted to say was, *I don't live here, either. I'm lost and I'm frustrated and I don't know where I belong.*

Why aren't you listening.

Take me somewhere else.

I padded into the bathroom, closed the door, and turned on the tap, dunking my wrists into the cool water that trickled into the basin below. Glancing to the right, I picked up unopened bottles of complimentary toiletries, beautifully packaged and carefully placed, examining the shiny caps and matching labels that signified symmetry and uniformity in this spotless room. Everything in here looked pristine and faultless – its surfaces sparkled, the towels smelled like cedar – and yet, when I looked in the mirror, its reflection told a different story. I took two of my fingers and made a tiny salute as I massaged my gums – a hopeless attempt at dental hygiene in absence of a brush. My fringe had been swept out of place and when I tried to press it back down it sprung up again as if to say, *More fool you, I'll do as I please.* I tackled the smudges of mascara over my cheekbones next, taking a square of toilet paper, folding it into a triangular point, and dabbing away the shadows from under my eyes with licks of saliva.

When I returned to the bed next door, I spotted a faint smear of menstrual blood on the crumpled white sheets, a roll-over residue from yesterday's moult. His suitcase was propped up in the corner and my jacket hung on the back of the door. Why had I come here again, and why couldn't I leave? What was real in this room, and what was fantasy? I had picked the one person who was the farthest away from me, and I was aware of the distance, I knew he would leave. Maybe that's why I did it – not just once, but multiple times. I sometimes wonder if I was compelled to return in order to confirm what I saw as an inevitability. Departures make sense to me. He comes and he goes and I stare motionless on a mattress dreaming of infinite doors.

When I was a child, I liked to sit in the back seat of my dad's car and imagine that the moon outside was following us, as if my surroundings were tied to me and our Volvo, as opposed to the other way around. Sometimes I leapfrogged the trees. Other times I'd jump across the rooftops. Night-time can have that effect on a person, even in adulthood. You invent the things you want to see. You chase the moon. You vault over the facts. You push people away because you're afraid of letting them in. You ask to be held but maybe you want to be loved. You say, *I'm brave*, when what you're really thinking is, *I'm scared*. You reach for the door. You ache for a release.

In the coarseness of daylight, I grabbed my coat, left the hotel and walked to the bus stop. The air was brisk and I tightened the belt of my coat with a vigorous knot. It was 7.30am and the roads were deserted, the pavements were bare, save for a couple of whistling street cleaners who were sweeping cigarette ends and beer cans into a cleaning trolley.

When the double-decker bus finally crawled into view, I beeped my debit card against the reader, plodded up the stairs and sat down towards the front. There was a dryness in my mouth and a hollowness around my heart. I swept my tongue across my teeth, back and forth, trying to wipe away the over-night residue, but it remained stubbornly in place. When I looked out of the window, whizzing rooftops interspersed with familiar flashes from the past as the bus cruised down the main artery of the Strand. We paused outside the shiny, metallic entrance of the Savoy Hotel and my mind returned to 2013, when I'd sipped cocktails on my hen night in a flamboy-ant bar with gold alcoves and plush carpets. Five nights before that, my fiancé had lunged at me with a doorstop, a frightened samurai without any memory of who I was. At the Savoy I was the frightened one, except it didn't go with my beaded dress and the gilded walls, so I laughed and I joked and said, *Yes, let's have another one.*

When my keys turned in the front door, I headed straight for the bathroom, peeled off my clothes and climbed into the tub. If you stand in the right spot, the water cascades directly over your head, and when it splits in two it sounds like thunder in a drum. Droplets trickled down my arm and I mopped them away with a sponge. My hair made a squeaky sound as I lath-ered up shampoo and rinsed it out with my fingers, watching the soap suds whirlpool around my toes, disappearing down the drain. Reaching over for a towel, my hand instinctively grabbed the plastic grooves of a safety rail drilled into the ceramic tiling that bordered the bath, and I instantly recoiled from its touch.

'I don't want it,' he'd said – but want and need are two separate things. Words echoed with the rain. I levered the shower handle and the pattering stopped.

The pattering never stops. There's no lever to control your thoughts – a pull for *on* and a push for *off* – although, mea culpa, I've often tried. Maybe I'll always carry her inside me, that young girl who sat quietly in the back seat of her father's car, looking out onto treetops and moonlight and magicking them into something else because the alternative isn't quite as poetic. Reality rarely is. Sometimes a door is just a door. You wake up in a bed that isn't yours with a loneliness so deep you hope it might be something else – but the handle twists, the man turns away, and the hallway leads you back the way you came.

I don't know why I hide the things that hurt me, not just from others, but from myself, in that hollow space around my heart. I think it has something to do with fear – of being exposed, of being seen – and maybe these two things are the same, but maybe they're not. Despite everything I've been through, I still can't tell you which it is.

Part IV

A I R

We tell ourselves stories in order to live.

— Joan Didion, *The White Album*, 1979

TEN

The kitchen window looked out onto grass and trees and a sky so voluminous my camera struggled to capture it within its oblong frame. Vast swathes of purple clouds puffed and swirled on top of powder blue, bordered below by a silhouette of forestland that seemed etched upon the horizon; a splattering of blood orange, fluorescent yellow and dazzling white light burned in the distance. A blazing fire of setting sun.

'That'll do,' I joked, reaching over to my wine glass and taking a sip of cava, as my friend Cila dunked greasy plates into the sink and rinsed them clean again, stacking them beside her cat, Isis, who was staking out her territory just like she always did. Isis was lithe and nimble and she knew it, patrolling the cupboards and worktops, a fortification she deemed well within her jurisdiction, weaving through soapy puddles, pawing at abandoned dishcloths and inspecting discarded vegetable peelings, before leaping onto the floor and sashaying away.

When I watched Cila tidying away the pots and pans, I was reminded of my grandmother and her outlines, contours that are forever in motion for me. As a child I would often observe her from afar: back turned, shoulders stooped, her hands busying themselves in the act of making and doing as she chopped and talked and washed. Her kitchen window overlooked a railway line where commuter trains screeched and clattered past her top floor apartment, hurtling towards some unknown destination, and I wonder whether she thought about that at all as she sponged the crockery, speaking of all the places she desired to see but never did.

The bedtime stories my grandmother told me always began on a path that took us into the woods. When I looked at Cila's front lawn, I couldn't help but notice a narrow trail that cut the grass in two, disappearing into the opaque trees beyond it, towards the blinding light, leading the eye somewhere else. Or at least that's what I'd always been told – that the path takes you somewhere – but for all our twilight adventures I have no memory of going on a single journey with my grandmother. Which is strange, because when I think of her it is the sound of vibrating railway tracks that I hear.

Memories and sensations aren't always linked together in a perfect paper chain. I had acquired some new ones over the last nine months but I didn't know how to connect them to my past life in a way that made sense to me. It was June and I was more confused than I had ever been, which probably explains why I found myself at the airport again, boarding a flight, this time to Santiago de Compostela in the north-west region of Spain. A few months previously, Cila had moved from the craggy, mountainous peaks of Andalucía to the fresh, luscious valleys of Galicia and was now renting a remote house in a quiet corner of A Coruña, surrounded by farmland and treetops and drizzling clouds. It gave the air the kind of earthy scent that two scientists in the 1960s called 'petrichor', a word that is soused in mythology, partly inspired by the Greek word 'ichor', which refers to the golden liquid that flows through the veins of the gods.

I forage for stories, just like my grandmother did, but mine were running away from me that summer, like I knew they eventually would. Experimentation had led to uncertainty and doubt. One step forward, two steps back. I hurried through the departure lounge with an exasperation that had very little to do with airport travel, seething at the security queue, tutting at loitering travellers who, as far as I could tell, were faffing about just to get in my way. A woman ambled ahead of me at a leisurely pace, talking about hedgehogs with her husband, and I let out a passive-aggressive sigh as I barged past them with nowhere particularly to go, no aeroplane to rush to board. I was infernally angry but I didn't seem to know it, which is the worst kind of feeling because you tend to throw it like hand grenades at minor situations and unsuspecting members of the public just to get it *out* and *away*. Reaching into my hand luggage, I rummaged around for my iPhone charger and pulled out my vibrator cable cord instead.

'I just realised I brought my vibrator USB instead of my iPhone charger,' I texted Zoë as I stood in the middle of the bustling concourse. 'You know, for the vibrator that's broken? Could this get any more Freudian?'

I sat down in the airport lounge and dropped my bag on the floor. I was beginning to unravel.

'It's okay if you enjoyed it,' my friend had commented a few days after I'd peeled myself away from that hotel bed.

'Enjoyed what?' I replied – knowing full well what she was referring to.

I could hear a flurry of exchanges in my head, between one version of myself and the other, but none of them seemed to provide me with any particular answers. I thought sex would present me with at least one, but if anything it seemed to spawn more distrust in myself and the choices I was making. I'd let another person in, I'd rocked myself against a new idea, and now I was sitting on another uncomfortable chair in yet another waiting lounge, asking myself what constitutes change. I had recently read about the aquatic salamander that can regrow lost limbs after injury, cell by cell, a phenomenon that one scientist commented could help us mimic a similar kind of repair in humans. The salamander can even reproduce heart tissue, interlacing and re-patterning myocardiocyte cells in the muscle layer. A resurrected heart, imagine that.

I absent-mindedly curled my headphone wire around my fingers in a looping pattern whilst I waited for my flight to be called. The passenger terminal was empty, but the airfield was active and engaged. Catering trucks zigzagged across the concrete, delivering food and drinks for the flight. A tow tractor sidled into a berth. Baggage handlers in high-vis tabards grabbed at handles and swung cumbersome luggage onto a rotating conveyor belt. Bags and cases disappeared into the hold. I followed two aeroplanes as one took off and another landed, a criss-cross of aluminium wings that cut against the peppery sky. I used to do this in the hospital car park as I ate my lunch. I'd sit on a wall and look up into the expanse that stretched from left to right, following the vapour trails, tracing the lattice of dissolving paths with squinting eyes. Sometimes it is easier to stare at contrails in the sky than it is to track the pathways of your own thoughts and consider what it means to be the one left behind.

Does involuntary desertion still count as abandonment? It certainly felt that way, although I hadn't allowed myself to contemplate its weight and form up until now. Who wants to own that? Who wishes to carry it? Abandonment is the oldest fairy tale trope in the book. The Brothers Grimm canonised it. Angela Carter subverted it. Charles Dickens dressed it in the musty folds of satin, lace and silk. In his novel *Great Expectations*, a jilted spinster sits in a crumbling mansion, goading time, daring it to feast on her in a long white veil and a scattering of jewels. When a young Pip first encounters Miss Havisham, he sees, in those first moments, both a waxwork and a skeleton, and is part-bewitched and part-repulsed by the ashes and effigy and bone. There are no working clocks at Satis House and the moth-eaten lady has not quite finished dressing, one shoe on, the other on the cobwebbed banquet table beside an uneaten bridal cake, near the half-moon of her withered hand.

'Do you know what I touch here?' she said, laying her hands, one upon the other, on her left side.

'Yes, ma'am.'

'What do I touch?'

'Your heart.'

'Broken!'

How realistic is cardiac regeneration when the damaged parts connect you to a past you can't quite let go of? Miss Havisham is nearly always played as an older woman in televised versions of Dickens' novel, but within the pages of *Great Expectations* she is in her mid-thirties, just like me. Stories are always subject to adaptation, even the exalted ones, but I wonder what this particular tweak says about the ways in which age and gender play into such depictions of grief, and more specifically, a woman's pain. Perhaps Miss Havisham's bitterness is more acceptable in an older guise – less threatening, easier to caricature – but I suspect that her age adjustment has more to do with a certain male fantasy of a woman who is so broken by her love that she sacrifices herself to one man, and one man alone, for the rest of her life. By cranking up the age of Miss Havisham, this kind of gender-specific fidelity isn't just accentuated, it's intensified, because we can very obviously *see* the passing of every decade in her greying hair and wrinkled skin. Miss Havisham has become a perfect embodiment of the woman who waits, and waits, until it is too late to turn back; a virginised fetishisation of female abandonment that plays into a very outdated, Victorian stereotype.

It has been suggested that Dickens' ghostly invention was based on a 30-year-old woman in Newtown, Sydney; an unsubstantiated claim to accompany an unverified tale of heartbreak – another virginised fetishisation of a woman who waits and waits. Eliza Donnithorne was born at the Cape of Good Hope in 1821; on the morning of her wedding day, she waited for her fiancé at the assembled breakfast, but he never arrived. These are the facts. If you Google her name, like I did, you'll find a Wikipedia page that lists her occupation as 'recluse'. There is the myth. Thirty years a hermit, or so the story goes. Legend has it that when the guests departed, Eliza pulled down the blinds and chained her front door – an anchorite in her perennial wedding dress, or to quote a local Australian newspaper report 60 years after her death, 'a woman in whom hope had died'. But if you ask me, that's just another invention, because how do you certify the death of hope? There's no gravestone for that; there's no post-mortem for despair.

In *Angela Carter's Book of Fairy Tales*, Carter likens stories to seeds that plant themselves from place to place, not because we necessarily share all the same experiences, but because 'stories are portable', we carry them with us, they are 'part of the invisible luggage people take with them when they leave home'. I thought about this as I waited for my plane. Miss Havisham was never a widow and yet to all intents and purposes she may as well have been, and I think that I carried this strange woman inside me somewhere in the back of my mind: the shrunken contours of a paralysing grief disintegrating into powder – an image of a woman I didn't want to be.

Was this ghost story even an appropriate one for me to carry? I hadn't been abandoned, my husband had been taken against his will, and yet the emotional pain felt uncannily similar. I feared my own vulnerability, so I pushed it away. I banished my wedding dress to my mother's house and she shut it away inside my childhood wardrobe along with a shoebox of old photos and my father's coats and shirts. I tried to do that with my feelings, too, but you can only box them up for so long. My overwhelming motivation up until this point was a pretty basic one: I didn't want to be pitied; I didn't want to be defined by my grief.

However, it isn't so easy extricating yourself from the stories you've been fed for so long. I was wrestling with the limitations of language and narrative, with the storylines I had passively absorbed growing up, the sexist tropes: tales of captive princesses, cannibalistic witches and spurned stepmothers. The abandoned woman is just another variation on this theme. Picture Homer's devoted Penelope, the immortal prototype of womanly patience and marital fidelity, weaving her loom and rejecting suitors' advances as she waits for her long-lost husband, Odysseus, to return to her. Which he does, of course, as if Homer is rewarding his creation for her loyalty, virtue and good grace. We revere these qualities in women, and we exalt them in those who grieve, too. Many times I was praised for my poise and dignity, compliments that both comforted and riled me, because whilst they promoted an image that appealed to me – the idea of decorum as strength – they also boxed me in, leaving little room in my broken heart for clutter and mess.

Some days I tried to augment these qualities, other days I kicked against them, fuelled by what I perceived to be others' objectification of my grief. For my thirty-sixth birthday I bought a floor-length silver dress and spiralled around the dance floor to the bump and grinds of T. Rex, shrieking and laughing with friends, bouncing up and down as if with every *thump* to the ground, I was hammering the idea of the jilted spinster, and her musty lace, into the concrete below. The silver dress was simply another way to inhabit a different role for a few hours, much like the red boots I bought for my husband's funeral. They were markers that signalled that I wasn't a widow who could be pinned down, a narrative that gave me hope as I returned to the modern, subversive fairy tales I had begun to read when my husband was in hospital – stories like Angela's Carter's 'The Company of Wolves', her red-hooded woman in the woods, who laughs at her canine aggressor before peeling off her clothes and throwing them into the fire. Only, how does a widow flirt with the ferocious wolf without seeming demented or unhinged or – worse still – cold and insensitive? This question had still percolated even when I was spinning around on that dance floor.

When the sun finally burned through the early morning haze, I drew back the curtains and opened my bedroom window. I heard Cila's voice before I saw her run.

'Romeo! Romeo!' she yelled as the door slammed behind her, rattling the window frame that I was leaning on above.

I watched her sprint across the garden towards the front gate of the house, dressing gown flapping behind her as she raced over the tall grass and onto the pavement. She dashed across the road that cut between her house and the dense woodland on the other side before disappearing into the tall pine trees. A few minutes passed, followed by ten more, then I saw her re-emerging from the bushy thicket with a dishevelled cat in her arms. For the rest of the day, Romeo loitered by the door, hovering at the threshold, licking his grazed paws. Cila had found him stuck in the brambles, frozen and unable to move, and had managed to dislodge him, but it had taken a few determined tugs, and the rescue had left him jittery and confused. Later that day, I sat on the bench outside and spotted him crouched behind a flower pot, staring up at me apprehensively. *You and me both,* I thought, as I stroked him gently under his chin, taking a sip of wine, looking out towards treetops that had inspired one cat's daring escape into the unknown.

We craft our stories and we motion them into the air. They move around us, drifting and gliding with the pollen and spores, ascending with the breeze. I felt them hovering around me as I looked out towards the hilly peaks that scattered the horizon like distant crowning jewels. A cat looking for adventure. A widow tussling with love. I was convinced that Romeo's escapade held some kind of meaning for me, in the same way that I had persuaded myself that Miss Havisham was a cautionary tale I needed to side-step. I fixated on cats and wedding dresses because I didn't want to acknowledge the reality as I approached the first anniversary of my husband's death. It was a marker I feared. Nearing the end of a year of firsts – Christmas, New Year, my birthday shortly followed by his, our anniversary – I felt anxious as to what came next, as if the egg timer were on its last dissolving sand particles and it was time to flip it and start again.

After years spent armouring myself, the chinks were starting to appear. I wasn't just missing my husband anymore, I was missing the touch of someone else, a carnal realisation that made me feel not just alone – but lonelier than I had ever thought possible.

My moods began to rocket and dip with a similar volatility to the previous year, peaks and troughs which seemed less acceptable to me so near to my second autumn as a widow, surely a time when I should be consolidating, not stumbling, looking to the sky for answers, hearing whispers in every gust of wind. How much longer would I keep yo-yoing like this? What had I learned? And, if I was unhappy with this latest iteration of myself, then who, exactly, did I want to be?

'There's no Grammy for grief, Kat,' my counsellor had levelled at me a few weeks earlier, much to my embarrassment. I was embarrassed because she was right. I knew that there was no perfect way to grieve, and yet I was picking and prodding at myself because things weren't playing out in the ways I hoped they would. Which isn't to say that I was expecting a happy ending here – I wasn't that much of a Pollyanna – but I was hopeful for an upwards trajectory that might take me further away from my grief and closer towards a new life as an enlightened widow, an elevated observation deck where I could look out from my vantage point and say to myself: *Yes, that's where I was then, but look at where I am now.*

The screenwriter John Yorke explores the tripartite form in his storytelling book *Into the Woods*: the set-up, the confrontation and the resolution. What appears to be, at first glance, a chaotic structure is actually a fractal construction beneath the surface: 'an extraordinarily ordered world that lies just underneath the appearance of freedom and chaos'. I had imbibed stories in order to both inhabit my experience and escape from it, and now I was confused because fantasy and reality weren't matching up. Where was this tidy structure in my own life? I wasn't sure what my life was centred around anymore. What was my purpose? Although this may sound strange, I had found structure in the trauma of a six-year illness. Take away one and the other evaporates, too. I think I even missed it sometimes, the fear, as if it was an addiction that my body still craved, like nicotine. I used to joke that I excelled in chaos, but what if this were genuinely the case? What if anarchy were a state I actually preferred?

The truth was that I didn't feel equipped to deal with everyday life because it didn't really make sense to me. One minute you're on your hands and knees on a supermarket floor, begging your husband not to die, and the next you're at the delicatessen counter in the same store, only it's three years later, your husband *has* died, and you're shouting at a Sainsbury's employee because none of their pre-packaged meat caters for one.

I had spent years in a state of constant emergency, my mobile phone placed next to my laptop at work in anticipation of yet another seizure that would wrench me away from my daily routine. My identity had been wrapped around an intention, it had been consumed by one sole purpose – the fight to survive. There is little time or space to consider the intricacies of your own self-consciousness when a brain tumour is ravaging the person you love. My two main jobs were to protect and maintain, and for a long time they defined the woman I was – and the wife others saw.

Unique situations can bring out extreme traits in a person that can make them seem infallible to those watching on. It even has a name: hysterical strength. Extreme feats that are performed by everyday people in life-and-death situations. *The Incredible Hulk*'s co-creator, Jack Kirby, referenced it as an influence on the superhero's form, citing the day he witnessed a mother lifting a car chassis off her trapped child.

To those around us, my husband and I were as superhuman as a hulking, green Goliath levering a 4,000-pound Jeep with our bare hands – but adrenaline had played into this myth as much as anything else. I'm not sure I could take any credit for a biological mechanism I had very little control over. My adrenal glands had done most of the work. Without a tumour to chase, less heroics were needed, which meant there was more opportunity for me to fail and disappoint – or at least that's how I perceived it. I wondered what everyone would make of me if they knew the truth. That I couldn't go to bed at night without checking the controls on the oven hob once, twice, then three times. That I couldn't even *say* the word cancer because it tasted sour in my mouth like lumpy milk. That I hit my face sometimes when I couldn't sleep. That after eight months of living alone, I still couldn't bring myself to eat my dinner at the kitchen table. That I smashed my printer on the kitchen floor simply because it ran out of ink.

I was waiting for an inevitable fall from grace. How had I been able to handle horrific, life-altering events and yet here I was, stumbling over quotidian things? It felt ridiculous to me – as if I were a retired guerrilla fighter haemorrhaging on a paper cut in the comfort of my own home. I could handle the A&E calls, and the epileptic seizures, and the IVF needles, but what I couldn't deal with was the banality and monotony of flatlined days and insipid routines. When my husband was ill, I had prayed for days like these, but now they were here I didn't know what to do with them, each one as translucent as the next.

I was tired of simply existing. The heartache after heartbreak is all the things you long for but can't quite visualise – only you're desperate for them anyway and the frustration keeps you awake at night. You're left wanting. To be pulled and kneaded. Plunged into and stretched out, all silky and soft, pushed down and outwards with the heels of two hands. Then folded and turned until your sinews are lengthened like elastic. I craved movement, momentum, provocation, even. I had found it again stroking new skin under hotel sheets, but it couldn't be sustained.

'You're angry,' my counsellor said, when I returned to the UK.

'Am I?' I replied.

'Yes – and you don't even know what to do with it.'

ELEVEN

Someone once told me – no doubt channelling Massive Attack – that love is a verb. I first met Richard Ratcliffe in 2017, exactly a year before my husband died, outside the Iranian Embassy in South Kensington. He set me to work straight away, handing me a piece of chalk and instructing me to write his wife's name on the pavement outside. A cluster of yellow balloons had been attached to a nearby tree with golden ribbon. As the light began to fade into dusk, remembrance candles were lit and small padlocks were scattered on the tarmac around photographs of a young mother and her child. I reached for my Dictaphone and began to record.

'Do vigils like this work?' I asked.

Richard quietly pondered the question before answering.

'It doesn't matter,' he replied. 'I know it's what Nazanin wants. She needs to know that I've stood by her side.'

I had been sent to Kensington Gardens to report on a tale of heartbreak. Eighteen months previously, Richard's wife, Nazanin Zaghari-Ratcliffe – a British-Iranian dual citizen – had been arrested at Tehran's Imam Khomeini airport by members of Iran's elite Revolutionary Guard as she was boarding a flight home to London with her two-year-old daughter. Nazanin, travelling on a dual passport, had taken Gabriella to meet her grandparents for the first time. On the day I first met Richard, it had been 544 days since he had seen his wife and child. Nazanin had been imprisoned on 'non-specific' charges and sent to Evin Prison in north-western Tehran. No one knew when he would get to see his family again.

'She made this,' he said quietly, reaching into his pocket to show me a small woodblock carving. When I looked down at his cupped hand, I made out its form: two figures cradling their child, hands clasped together as the mother's hair enveloped around them like Hokusai waves.

'That's me, that's her – and that's Gabriella,' he said, smiling.

Nazanin had made it for Father's Day.

How many stories of loss can one embassy car park hold? The day before this interview, my husband and I had paid £450 for an intrauterine insemination package that had failed – a less invasive fertility procedure that involves directly inserting washed sperm into the womb at the most fertile point during a menstrual cycle, a precise science that still involves trans-vaginal scans, hormone injections and flexible catheters. So really, define 'invasive'. My husband had completed his latest chemotherapy treatment ten days previously. Three 28-day cycles of a drug called Temozolomide, a drug that, ironically, initiated more epileptic seizures, and left him feeling drained, nauseous and breathless.

Some reporting jobs get under your skin. Although I was unaware at the time, I would closely follow Richard and Nazanin's story from this day forward, writing several more reports, the last filed in May 2018, only three months before my husband died. There was something about their separation that struck a chord with me, something about the mixture of hopefulness and frustration I saw in Richard that I kept returning to because it seemed to resonate with my own.

The day after I arrived in A Coruña, Richard began a hunger strike outside the Iranian embassy. I kept up to date with what was happening from Cila's house in Spain, sending texts to Richard and reading news apps, but I was agitated by the distance. I felt too far removed from what was happening at home, and as the days went by, Richard's self-inflicted famine occupied my thoughts more and more. On the morning that I flew back to London, I booked a taxi home, dumped my suitcase in the kitchen, and headed straight out again, bound for West London on an empty District Line train. There was no report to write this time, no Dictaphone to switch on, no editor to file to. Much like the grief that had consumed me, I had crossed over an invisible line where I was now a witness, not a reporter, observing the minutiae around me without knowing exactly where to put it.

I visited Richard most days during that two-week strike. As the days multiplied, so did the multicoloured Post-It notes with messages from concerned visitors that dappled the metal barriers, a barricade of corrugated fencing that Iranian embassy officials had erected. Another imposed separation – only this one could be seen and photographed, a tangible emblem decorated with a mosaic of words such as *hope* and *free* and *home* and *strength*. A woman called Susie had written three bars of a Scottish ballad onto her yellow square. I watched the comings and goings from the sidelines, silently observing the myriad journalists who stood awkwardly in clusters with their camera crews, most of them politely declining to wear the *Free Nazanin* badges that were being distributed by volunteers. *Partiality* and *objectivity*, they said. Over the coming days, politicians came and went, standing stiffly in line to converse with a starving man. One morning I watched a distracted MP glance at his watch impatiently, as his assistants swiped at their phones around him. Behind him was a woman who had travelled for hours to be here. She had read about Richard's plight in the paper and felt compelled to physically journey to London, and when she stood beside the patchwork altar of Post-It notes she cried genuine tears as she read from left to right, a pilgrim who had journeyed to a holy place where grief was sleeping rough in a two-person camping tent.

Most days I stood and watched, fixated on the ever-diminishing body that sat in front of me, a face that was becoming gaunt and haggard, and yet there was a sturdiness there that made me feel little pity, only awe and wonder at the ways in which he was seizing his own story and demanding that others listen. If you were to have asked me that week what love looked like, I would have replied that it resided there in that fold-out picnic chair, and sometimes when I looked at its gaunt form it pulled at the frayed edges of my own heart. I had avoided it because I wasn't sure how to acknowledge the tear. A broken heart suggests a brittle material, but I know that my cone-shaped organ is made from muscle and sinew and blood. You can slice cardiac tissue but it cannot snap in two. It isn't made of glass and it cannot float like wood. There are no gaps between my ventricles, and yet, standing on the tarmac day after day outside that embassy, I felt the breeze ruffle between them like gossamer sheets.

How do you assign words to a rip that you feel in everything you do? In the process of approving a recent broadsheet essay, I had asked for the word 'soulmate' to be removed from a photograph caption without even knowing why. All I knew was that it bothered me and I wanted it erased. It was a categorisation that seemed to add weights to my ankles and, in all honesty, I wasn't sure what it even meant. True to form, my agitation led me to further research. I began reading about animals that mate for life. Geese who mourn in isolation. Coyotes who never stray. Sandhill cranes who call to each other in a synchronised duet. Mute swans are ascribed as such because they are less vocal than other species and yet I have heard one call loudly for its lost mate, a high pitched squeak without a returning yowl to soothe the bird's distress.

What happens when you come to the realisation that all the stories you ever told yourself are no longer viable? In the summer of 1968, Joan Didion checked herself into an outpatient psychiatric clinic at St John's Hospital, after experiencing an attack of vertigo and nausea that left her questioning the flimsy line between conception and reality. She had just been named *Los Angeles Times*' 'Woman of the Year'. In twelve months' time, a group of radicalised hippies would go on the rampage in Los Angeles, brutally killing nine people and signalling a gruesome end to an ambiguous decade of love. A sense of foreboding stalks the opening chapters of *The White Album*, a collection of essays that was published eleven years later in 1979. It's a foresight Didion gives herself with retrospection, and it becomes a part of her own story, as conception and reality join forces in order to tell it – a time when she began doubting her own narrative line.

'I was supposed to have a script, and had mislaid it,' she writes. 'I was supposed to hear cues, and no longer did. I was meant to know the plot, but all I knew is what I saw: flash pictures in variable sequence, images with no "meaning" beyond their temporary arrangement, not a movie but a cutting-room experience.'

Similarly to Didion's, my life had become a scattering of Polaroids on my kitchen table, piles of intermingled memories that could take a lifetime to place in order. Overwhelmed by the sheer quantity of them, I became my own movie editor, picking up memory after memory, raking over them with what I intended to be an objective eye, but it quickly became a subjective gaze, leaving me questioning the 'amazing carer' epithet that others had so enthusiastically assigned to me.

On a Wednesday evening in late June, I sat on my sofa in tears with my friend Andy and admitted that I wasn't sure if I had been a sufficient carer. I wasn't convinced I had been good enough. There were times when my frustrations got the better of me, they snatched the best parts of me. When my husband's short-term memory crumbled, I'd sometimes snap when I had to repeat something for the third or fourth time. One evening, I threw a potato I had been peeling at the kitchen wall for no particular reason other than I wanted to hurl something somewhere and a root vegetable seemed as good a missile as any.

On the evening of his second stroke, only two days after he had returned home from St Christopher's Hospice, I asked him to open the front door to his sister because I was simultaneously cooking dinner and washing laundry and I was on the verge of cracking after a day in which I'd had to confiscate his debit card and keys because he couldn't remember that it was too dangerous for him to wander around our neighbourhood alone. He collapsed as he opened the door and I blamed myself for the stroke that followed. I blamed myself for a lot of things. I didn't want him to die at home. Neither did he, but that no longer consoled me. And then there was the IVF, a particular chapter in my life that was so ambiguous it still haunted me.

A few days after my in vitro embryo transfer, it felt like my body was rejecting the whole premise – that we could try for a family like everyone else – and I began to panic. I didn't feel in control of what was happening, and my husband was becoming more and more distant, detached from the things I was telling him. He sat quietly as I described how the progesterone pessaries, the hormone supplements I had to insert twice a day in order to artificially thicken my uterine lining, were making me ill, a burning pain that tightened around my ribs and throbbed down my back.

One evening, the acid reflux became so acute that I doubled up in pain and we ended up in A&E because I could no longer walk. It was heartburn on an unprecedented scale, and the symbolism wasn't lost on me as we sat in an empty hospital corridor and waited for an on-call gynaecologist to palpate and scan me. I lay quietly in the hospital bay and tried to summon the strength to voice my concerns to the consultant, but every time I opened my mouth to speak it refused to move, as if the muscles around my lips were as wearied as the rest of me.

The longer I lay there in silence, the more I wondered whether those muscular fibres were guarding me from saying the truth out loud, lest I be misinterpreted or judged or queried. It was midnight in this emergency department and I wanted to stop the clock, not to turn back time but to freeze it so I could suspend myself in the air around me. If I could create a motionless world, silent and still, then maybe I would be able to start feeling the movements inside me again, maybe I would be able to sense the water and the hydrogen atoms and the millions of cells, dividing and reproducing at this very moment, as I lay on this hard mattress wishing to disappear. I was tired of the pain, and the waiting, and the man sitting beside me seemed to be lost in a faraway place I no longer had a map for. What kind of hope was this? The next morning, I reached for a pessary before returning it to its box unopened. And the next day. And the day after that. Was it sabotage or aiding? Sometimes in life, it can be both.

Stories aren't static. They divide and duplicate, just like the trillions of transforming cells that voyage within us. The ancient Greeks revered their mythology because it helped explain the unexplainable. Love and grief. War and death. A crescent moon that hangs in the night sky. The thunder above and the quaking below. The tides of the sea and the scattering of the constellations. Heroes and allegorical creatures that gave actions, words and meaning to all the elements and phenomena that they wished to understand.

Although my husband was a pragmatic man, he came to believe that a raven had portended his brain tumour. His story went something like this: years before we met, he had returned to his Stoke Newington flat one Sunday afternoon and, upon entering his bedroom, had jumped at the sight of a colossal black wing quivering and flopping underneath the duvet covers, ebony feathers struggling to shake off his cotton sheets. The bird had somehow flown in through an open window, and in its disorientated state, was unable to find its way back out again. He referenced this story more frequently as the oligo-astrocytoma expanded and contracted to the whim of his own biological chemistry. He began reading Edgar Allan Poe.

'Once upon a midnight dreary, while I pondered, weak
  and weary,
Over many a quaint and curious volume of forgotten
  lore—
While I nodded, nearly napping, suddenly there came a
  tapping,
As of some one gently rapping, rapping at my chamber
  door.
"'Tis some visitor," I muttered, "tapping at my chamber
  door—
Only this and nothing more."'

Poe's narrative poem 'The Raven' spoke to my husband in the same way that *Great Expectations* now speaks to me. When life contorts, you begin looking for meaning, and an open page is as good a spot as any, like an Enigma machine for the soul. In Poe's gothic rhyme, a nameless man sits by a dwindling fire, reading stories in order to try to forget the death of his lost Lenore. Watching the dying embers, his reading is interrupted by a tapping outside, and when he opens his windows a raven swoops into his chamber, a talking creature whose repetitious 'nevermores' come to signify one man's desolate grief. This poem is a requiem without absolution. An ambiguous meditation on the nature of love and loss and the warring elements that can imprison a person.

In Norse mythology, the one-eyed god Odin is often depicted alongside two ravens, Huginn and Muninn, that fly around the world gathering information, whispering observations to their master, regaling him with faraway tales of what they have heard and what they have seen. Translated from Old Norse, these two ravens' names mean *thought* and *memory*; when my husband's began to fade, he held on to the feathered wings of fantasy in order to create a world where flying birds bring messages home from a far-flung land in the future.

I watched two ravens take flight from a hospice room window. On the day that they disappeared, nurses came and went in a flurry of intermittent activity that encircled the bed where he lay. That afternoon, our last together, paralysis turned to panic as reality commandeered the myth. He slipped in and out of consciousness, attempting to speak, but the morphine slurried his words into a watery mixture that had no recognisable structure or form. Liquid thoughts splattered and sploshed, lapping against the walls and puddling under his bed before evaporating into the air. I salvaged what I could, but he was drifting between two worlds now, a holding space where thoughts and memories were airborne, hovering above the wheelchair and the walking frame and the wife who was curled on the chair by his feet.

In a last-ditch attempt to catch a handful of his departing neurons, I asked him to list his favourite books. 'Why now?,' he asked. And I didn't have the courage to reply, *Because if not now – when?* In his final weeks, I had witnessed his body harden and contract, encasing him, day by day, much like a fragile songbird within a metal cage. Five months previously, he had begun writing a book about the science of memory and consciousness, exploring the destabilising impact his tumour had on what he called 'the invisible chambers of the mind'. He named it *Among a World of Ghosts*. On the day he died, the perimeters of that world ran to 60 pages. 18,000 words.

Over those six weeks of summer, I witnessed the dissipation of a bright soul. When his hands were unable to grasp the ink channel of a ballpoint pen, he began to dictate fragments of prose, sentences he had memorised, that splattered the page like modernist poetry. On his final day, I held his iPad and read his broken text as if it was a sacred psalm.

'History is a loaded term

A series of stories aeeanged thematically

I'm 41 mnoqnow subject to frequent hallucinations and absences seizures fits too shaky to walk dress up as propped up in a hospital bed jabbing one fingered st w nottowwedipad amid a mound of improving literature and biscuit t crumbs.'

He dictated his final contribution with only hours left to live. When I'd finished typing, I photographed his notes on my iPhone. An instinctive motion. A desperate attempt to capture the last electrical firings of a brilliant mind.

'Each individual brain is shaped differently,' he told me, through gritted teeth, as the morphine battled with his pain receptors. 'Individuals are different. And, uniquely amongst bodily organs, the human brain has the ability to reshape, repair and reorder itself in the face of damage, trauma or injury.'

These were some of the final words he uttered. In the summer of 2019, I read them again and again. I had vowed to finish his book and, true to form, I had romanticised this pledge, reading about Mary Shelley's life after the death of her husband, Percy Bysshe Shelley, who drowned on the north-western coast of Italy when she was 24 years old. Over the next year, she reanimated his work desk, combing through fragments of poetry scribbled on the back of envelopes and scraps of jumbled paper. Collaborating with him beyond the grave, she pieced his stanzas together, remnant by remnant, producing a patchwork quilt of verse that was published in 1824, two years after his death, titled *Posthumous Poems*.

It is said that when Percy Shelley's drowned body was cremated on a beach in Tuscany, his heart refused to burn on the blazing pyre, and when his friend Edward Trelawny reached into the smouldering embers, he recovered the defiant organ, later giving it to Mary who kept it in a keepsake box inside her writing desk, wrapped in silk along with a handful of ashes and a copy of his poem, 'Adonais', until her own death in 1851.

I thought of Adam Pilarz tucked into the drawer of my grandmother's dressing table when I read this. There are other ways to hold on to a heart. I thought that it could be done by raking and sifting through the last vestiges of my husband's deliberations, but the reality had sharper edges to it than sinew, ashes and silk. I had been left with a wreckage I couldn't reconstruct. Broken sentences, random words, trailing thoughts, obscure hyperlinks. Dreamlike prose that I had no hope of detangling in a way that would ever do it justice. I went through notepad after notepad of analysis and research with the intention of doing it – of telling his story – only to realise that it could only be narrated by the man who had written all these words down: my husband, the haunted storyteller, moving among a world of ghosts.

On the first day that I wandered into the Wellcome Library, I didn't really have a plan. I was simply looking for shelter. I picked a random chair amongst the books, unpacked a notepad, a pen and a laptop from my tote bag, and began writing things down. Notes at first. Disjointed sentences like my husband's. Splinters of feeling. Clusters of thoughts like *hands gripping* and *letting go* and *falling* and *I am scared of forgetting*. I had seen my husband grapple with his memory, I had watched him lose grip on his words as time ran out, and I needed to take hold of my own. I wrote random memories down on paper. Here is one:

'The year is 1986 and I am sitting cross-legged on a roundabout in my nursery playground. I have been told to keep two hands on the brightly coloured rails but a voice in my head wonders what might happen if I remove them both simultaneously, and so I do, I release my grip, falling backwards, my head hitting the tarmac.'

This memory is closely followed in my notebook by a statement on the next page: 'I can't drive.' There is no explanation – only a stream of random musings below it scribbled in black biro. At the bottom of the page, I reference astronauts who went and saw, and came back to a different planet. I have circled this sentence with an arrow that points to a single word that hovers on the lined page:

'Re-entry'.

I read to ascend, I wrote to return. If my story was, like Joan Didion's, a scattering of cutting-room images, then it was time to get on my hands and knees and explore them in situ – not to rearrange the past but to document what I saw. The first pages of this book began with me crouched down on the ground. It began at a point where I realised that I needed to let go of all the things I couldn't decipher into the rings of atmosphere above. Words can't erase the stabs and throbs, but they can help you to understand them. They have helped me to understand mine.

When I wrote at my kitchen table, I often heard my upstairs neighbour's child being cooed at by his grandmother: gentle sounds that reminded me of the earthly surroundings that I sought to return to as I began to excavate the past. My descent through the atmosphere rattled and hummed to the babble of a newborn above me. His gurgles echoed as the air began to cool, and when I reached for the parachute pull, the ground came into view.

TWELVE

When I was six years old, I sat an entrance exam for a school I had no interest in attending. I think that my mother must have subliminally known this because she completely forgot that she had arranged for me to take a test that day. She had forgotten to tell me, too. I remember sitting cross-legged on the classroom carpet, eagerly awaiting story time, when I spotted her zigzagging across the playground, looking for an unlocked door that would let her into the building, rattling the handle that led into our arts and crafts corner, and nearly tripping over a mop and bucket that had been left stranded in the middle of the room. She was flustered, I thought, more curious than alarmed. Even as she scooped me up and galloped us through empty corridors, buckling me into our car that was parked outside, panting, 'I forgot. We're late,' I observed her panic with a degree of titillation, as most six year olds would at 11am on a Wednesday morning when they have no idea what they're late for.

As memories go, it's a pretty sensory one: a fairly understandable childish urge to return to soft carpet as I was plonked down at an uncomfortable writing desk in a draughty hall. But not just any old writing desk, an antique flip-top writing desk that was attached to the seat by a wrought iron bracket. I shivered in my uniform as I watched the room fill up with girls in starched shirts and pleated skirts who took their seats with a quiet confidence that suggested they had a better understanding of why they were here and what they were expected to do at these wooden tables.

My seat felt hard and rigid and I wriggled my legs under the framework. Just a blank page in front of me and a sharpened pencil to my right. I placed my hand on the wooden surface and followed the timber grain like Braille with my thumb, feeling its irregular grooves whilst a solemn teacher paced up and down the central aisle, drawing our attention to a chalky sentence on the blackboard ahead of us. *Ah*, I thought, *so this is why we're here*. Each child was instructed to write a story inspired by this opening line and we had 45 minutes in which to do so. I squinted at the slate and folded my arms, unmoved by what I had to work with, underwhelmed with the words they had selected for us, and when the papers were collected at the end of our allotted time, I handed in a blank page with a confused mixture of both pride and embarrassment.

If there was an impudence at play that day, it wasn't intentional. I've always been reluctant to speak until I think I have something of worth to say. This occupied my thoughts as I began scribbling in the summer of 2019, and it only seemed to intensify as I resolved to turn these scribbles into a book, a tactile object that could be picked up, opened and flicked through, brought to life and preserved on the page. Only, how do you know when your words are ready to be harvested? Is it possible to gather them up without damaging them in some way? Come to think of it, what made mine any more salient than anyone else's? I kept thinking back to that six-year-old girl with a sharpened pencil in her hand, brimming with words, but unwilling to write them down until she was fully ready to let them go.

'You weren't chatty in the normal way,' my mother said to me recently, in reference to my early childhood. To which I replied, 'Define normal,' but I knew what she meant. I didn't start speaking until I was two-and-a-half years old. My grandmother was the first person to ring the alarm, taking my parents aside one day to inform them that I was too quiet and that, perhaps, they should look into my muteness.

In a house full of children, I tended to retreat into my own world, as far away from the banging and the squabbling as I could possibly get. Throughout my early childhood, I liked to sit under the kitchen table and listen to the adults who congregated around cups of tea, discussing subjects I had no way of ever understanding: serious matters such as marital strife, rising property prices, South African apartheid and the Berlin Wall. The exact meaning of what I was hearing didn't matter – which is just as well. We talk about harmonic cadence in musical theory, but there is rhythm and melody in conversation too, and I surfed the rise and fall under that table, absorbing words as if they were musical notes.

It is impossible to wholly theorise my reluctance to speak, although I like to think it signalled some kind of innate appreciation in me, a very early reverence for language, the way it can quiver down the segments of your spinal vertebrae, from cervical to thoracic to lumbar. My doctor, however, had other ideas – deafness being one – so I was sent to an early learning centre and asked to point to letters of the alphabet with a magical wand, which I did, much to their surprise and relief. 'It's all there,' my mother said to my grandmother. 'She's just taking her time.' I began talking in four-word sentences just shy of my third birthday.

In 1971, towards the end of the Apollo 15 moonwalk, the American astronaut David Scott performed a live demonstration on the lunar surface, and I have watched the grainy footage several times, resetting the video player bar and starting it all over again. Scott bounces into view in his globular helmet and spacesuit, holding a 30-gram falcon feather in his left hand and a 1.32-kilogram aluminium hammer in his right. Mission Controller Joe Allen described the demonstration as the 'Apollo 15 Preliminary Science Report' – an unexceptional title for an extraordinary spectacle on a pockmarked satellite that is roughly 238,800 miles away from earth. 'I guess one of the reasons we got here today was because of a gentleman called Galileo,' Scott proffers to his audience, 'who made a rather significant discovery about falling objects and gravity fields.' As the camera zooms out, Scott drops the feather and the hammer simultaneously and we watch both objects fall to the ground at exactly the same time.

Even science is subject to mythologisation. Despite being one of the most famous experiments in our history, no one is 100 per cent certain that a young Galileo Galilei even dropped two objects of differing mass from the Leaning Tower of Pisa in 1589. In fact, most are sure it couldn't have occurred due to the effects of air resistance – and yet we know that this story holds credible meaning in spite of this fiction. We know that, within a vacuum, free-falling objects descend with the same acceleration regardless of their mass.

It's a premise that appealed to a widow in a public library. The idea that mismatched objects which are released together fall at the same speed. Physicists and astronauts aren't the only ones who are capable of conducting experiments in order to test cause and effect. I probed and prodded from a young age. I wouldn't say it was precociousness exactly, but I definitely tested the boundaries, only, unlike the Apollo 15 crew, I wasn't always smart in my approach. Like the time that I opened the car door on the motorway, aged six, to see what would happen. Or the random afternoon that I decided to toss my beloved teddy bear, Henry, into my grandmother's fireplace in spite of everything I knew about combustion. I thought he might be invincible. It was a real kicker to discover that he wasn't. To this day, I still can't bear to look at his singed paw, which is why he no longer lives with me. Henry resides in a cardboard box in my parents' attic, a brutal casualty of my naivete and romanticism, but also a very early exhibit of my inquiring approach to things.

Nothing is static, everything is open to provocation and enquiry. At least, that's how it felt every morning that I wandered into the Wellcome Library and opened up my laptop amongst piles of books that ranged from Freudian psychoanalysis to gravitational-wave astronomy. There may be no such thing as a perfect vacuum, but when I first began to narrate my own story it began in a space that had to be devoid of all the things that had been dragging me down. In this instance, the elemental matter was the basic language of grief, words that didn't seem to express or embody the complexities and contradictions that had defined my experience of it. One weekday morning, I met with a 55-year-old widower in Westminster for a broadsheet essay I was writing about exactly this – the limitations of language. As we sipped our cappuccinos, he told me that it had been many years since his wife had died and yet he was still compelled to tell strangers on the Tube. In fact, he had done exactly this only a few days earlier. 'How do you explain that you have a girlfriend but also a wife?' he asked me, and the only answer I could offer was that I had none to give.

'I'm a widow, but he'll always be my husband,' I snapped at Andy about a week later. It didn't seem fair to me that our titles weren't equal anymore. His was fixed in the past and yet I had been assigned a title that shrink-wrapped me in an accredited grief that had no expiration date, a label that had been constructed by someone else in order to package me into someone containable and controllable, but the air was stifling me and I couldn't breathe. Every so often, an insignificant conversation, a benign anecdote, would puncture through this taut surface with a sudden *pop* that I couldn't control. One evening I used the word 'husband' and watched a stranger's gaze fix on my ringless left hand. Sights and sounds weren't matching up. I began to feel like an anomaly; worse still, an impostor in my own life. I began editing myself in public, but you can't null and void a decade of memories. Where do you put them? You can't resect the past with a surgical knife. On any given day, in any conversation that I had, my previous life might be evoked by a seemingly harmless exchange that pulled him – and us – back into the room. Silly things, trivial asides. Replies like, 'Oh, my husband and I went there – they do great Sunday roasts.' Or, 'Our bathroom taps are leaking.'

I.
Me.
My.
Mine.

I recited these possessive pronouns every morning as I stood in the shower scrubbing away at my skin. I began questioning the language I had been given to use. Words like *loss* and *passed*. I have used the former throughout this book and yet it often feels heavy and misshapen in the context of my grief. To lose implies a failure to hold on to something. It suggests a degree of carelessness on the part of the possessor – although, in the context of bereavement, define possession. I'm the proprietor of what exactly? I didn't own my husband, and love isn't a wallet that falls out of your pocket on your way to work. I have lost many things in my life – sentimental jewellery, house keys, a sense of direction – but I have never lost a person. I have walked away from them, and they have walked away from me, but I have never absent-mindedly mislaid someone and later wondered where they might be. Surely words like *wrench* and *tear* are more appropriate when discussing the death of a loved one and yet, even here, there are days when such words can feel like daggers in your mouth. Sharp and jagged and barbed. It was only when I looked to the origins of the word *loss* that I began to reclaim it in everyday conversation.

> From the Middle English 'los' meaning *damage, destruction, loss.*
> From the Proto-Germanic 'lusą' meaning *dissolution, break-up, loss.*
> From the Proto-Indo-European 'lews' meaning *to cut, sunder, separate, loose, lose.*

To dissolve, to destruct, to cut away. This is what we mean when we talk about loss. As an active word, *a word that moves*, it begins to make sense, but what about the other grief phrases? Expressions like *to pass away* or *to pass over* both use an everyday verb that intimates a route, a bridge, a voyage from one location to another, up and across and away. We talk about the dead being *beyond us* as if the afterlife is a physical spot in the future where our loved ones have set up camp ahead of the living, a cosmic colony in the ultimate void between *here* and *there*, between what we know and what we'd like to believe. I doubt there is any widow or widower who hasn't tried to conjure a palpable space where their partner might be waiting for them, irrespective of faith or belief. My passage is a river: a wide, sparkling boulevard of silver and blue. It ripples under a rowboat. He ebbs and flows in the water. I see his multitudes and I hear him speak. Sometimes I follow the river's flow, from my hand that dips between two solid banks, to the estuary that draws him towards its gaping mouth, a threshold beyond the measures of time where his mortal dust meets the sea, some particles settling into the claggy silt below, others evaporating into the rising air, forming wisps of cloud, leaving all of its impurities behind.

In Don DeLillo's 2001 novella, *The Body Artist*, a young widow is reunited with her husband in a small bedroom on the third floor of her house. It is a modern ghost story, a quiet meditation on the trauma of grief, and I read it in a single sitting on a summer's afternoon in my garden as the blackbirds swooped and warbled. Disconnected from the outside world, and the body she inhabits, Lauren Hartke finds an ageless figure sitting on the edge of a bed who speaks to her in strange, garbled prose. Lauren is the recipient of a new language in a desolate realm where connection and communion no longer makes sense. These disjointed words, this phantom visitor, occupy a temporal space that consumes her as she wanders from room to room in an empty house on the New England coast.

DeLillo calls them 'unadjusted words'. They are without rhythm or tempo. They are vagabond strays. Nothing Lauren hears is recognisable in its form because it has no form. All meaning has been sucked into a vortex where shape, structure and cadence are redundant components, because what does any of that mean in a world where you are struggling to live again? What use is syntax when you can't even find the words to express the depths of your loneliness? The more I read, the more I began to fuse with this fictional character, alone in a ghost house, watching the birds peck on the feeder outside her window, waiting for an apparition that might give her the words she needs in order to regain possession of herself.

Halfway through the book, Lauren begins to wonder whether she might be in need of a doctor, and when she calls her friend, the synthesised answering machine recording she hears seems to embody her disconnection like an interstellar transmitter.

'How strange the discontinuity,' DeLillo writes. 'It seemed a quantum hop, one word to the next. She hung up and called back. One voice for each word. Seven different voices. Not seven different voices but one male voice in seven time cycles. But not male exactly either. And not words so much as syllables but not that either. She hung up and called back.'

Up until this point, I had avoided listening to my husband's voice, favouring the whispering leaves in distant woods to the countless voicemail messages that were still logged on my iPhone, sitting there silently, waiting patiently for me to hover my thumb over his name and press *play*. Something about DeLillo's quantum hop answering machine encouraged me to do just that.

18 December 2015 duration: 00:17
17 February 2016 duration: 00.13
8 February 2017 duration: 00:06

I counted them first. There were sixteen in total, covering a time period of four years, the last voice memo left three months before he died. I clicked on the date, *7 May 2018*. It gave me a time – *13:17* – and I pressed on the symbol for loudspeaker, releasing his mellow tones into the air as if it were a phantasmal substance from an enchanted lamp.

'Oh, I'm amazed I got through. There's no reception here at all.'

My body began to shake. I stopped him here and went on to the next one: *18 December 2015 at 18:04*. There was no voice at first, only the sound of the wind, a blustery gale that distorted his voice as he battled against it. Struggling to decipher what he was saying, I snatched broken snippets like *London Bridge* and *Jubilee Line* and *Let me know where you're going to be* – quotidian fragments, and yet how strange that the latter seemed to be communicating something far greater as I skimmed and dipped into a past that was now unequivocally in the present.

'Let me know where you're going to be.'

These eight words circuited and looped. Over the coming months, they gave me something to aim for as I sat down to write my own story. I had spent the last year wandering through departure lounges and floating gardens, hotel bedrooms and chattering forests, looking for new discoveries, new experiences, that might reunite my sensory and linguistic spheres so that I could speak them freely, and now I was finally ready to say them out loud. Bolder still, I was determined to commit them to paper.

Psychiatrist and author Bessel van der Kolk describes the moment a person discovers their self through language as a epiphanic discovery. 'Communicating fully is the opposite of being traumatised,' he writes in *The Body Keeps the Score*, describing how our self-awareness is split into two branches: one that monitors the self through time and another that senses it in the present. The first is what he calls our 'autobiographical self', which assembles memories and past experiences into what he calls 'a coherent story'. 'This system is rooted in language,' he writes – a system that is subject to constant change as we tell and retell it over time, accessing it, performing it, changing our perspective as we assimilate new data and decide which versions of ourselves to put out into the world. The other branch is rooted in the here-and-now of physical sensations – a part of the brain that registers a different, internal truth. 'It is this second system that needs to be accessed, befriended and reconciled,' he writes.

It was time for me to make peace with the here-and-now which was, of course, both time present and time past. In order to reconcile myself with the woman who checked the oven hob five times before she went to bed, I had to reconcile myself with the woman who ran into the street on a late Friday evening crying, 'Help me, help me,' as her husband chased her with a three-foot doorstop and the neighbours twitched their curtains. Every time my big toe went numb, or my leg needled up and down, I reminded myself of the first time these sensations occurred, four years previously, in the middle of Peckham Rye, my hands splayed on the grass as I whimpered and bawled because our house couldn't be a home for my anguish and this triangular patch of green was the nearest space I could find.

In van der Kolk's world, the relationship between language and physical sensation is both vital and profound, and he uses the story of a young deaf-blind girl in Alabama in order to illustrate its restorative power after trauma. When Helen Keller was seven years old she was, in her own words, 'at sea in a dense fog', able to distinguish people only by the vibrations of their footsteps, unable to communicate without the 60 sign gestures that Keller and her family invented. It was only when 20-year-old Anne Sullivan, a partially blind teacher, arrived to tutor Keller on 5 March 1887, a day that Keller later christened her 'soul's birthday', that words entered her world like dapples of light in the pitch-black chambers of her personage. Her independence day began when she recognised the motions of her teacher's finger in the palm of her hand, spelling *w-a-t-e-r* over her creased lifelines, as her other hand felt a cool trickle under a water pump. 'The living word awakened my soul, gave it light, hope, joy, set it free!' Keller would write sixteen years later in her autobiography.

When I first began writing about my grief, it had only been 52 days since the event itself. When my gut and heart overpowered my brain, words darted around our house; visible in the dark and yet impossible to net, they flitted over my head and zipped between my legs. Most of the time, I had little desire to catch them. I watched each one impassively with my eyes, tallying them up, calibrating their movements, watching them from afar. They didn't all stick around. Some flew out from the open window. I dumped a handful in a bin bag along with my husband's old shirts. Others simply dissolved into the walls.

The ones that lingered became part of a new lexicon at a time when language was acute and critical and almost entirely concerned with what was happening in me. Bodily descriptors such as *lurch* and *clenched* and *squeezed* took on new meaning as my muscles tensed, my skin tingled and my right foot occasionally went numb. There was little autonomy in those early days. I didn't choose the language I used, it chose me. Tempestuous words such as *slopping* and *rocking* and *falling* seemed to inhabit me, pulsing through my right arm and blustering down into my thumb and index finger as I scribbled them onto the page.

There is a ventriloquism that occurs in those early days when grief takes up residence in you, but it can't last forever. Eventually these words lose their potency as weeks turn to months and you begin looking for new language with which to express the nuance of what you're feeling.

I reached for it on my tiptoes, I found it in the natural world. The murmuring of the trees and the foaming crests of breaking waves. The cracks in the earth and the vanishing ice of our towering glaciers. The ripples in space and the streams of dust in the tails of comets. Unpredictable cycles of change. I studied snowflakes and tree rings and butterfly cocoons until the air thinned around me and I began to reconcile with my present self, in all its wild and contradictory formations. After months of oblivion, I set my sights on self-determination and I released myself with language, only I would be the one who decided the words this time, seizing my story by writing it down.

Van der Kolk writes that we are phantoms until we find ourselves through language, although even that word is slightly ambiguous to me. We are all haunted by different things and each of these ghosts can take on any number of forms, shaped not by what we see so much as what we are seeking, whether that is absolution, or some kind of preservation, an extrication from reality, or a return to the here and now as we recreate the past in order to make our peace with the present. Some believe that phantoms are a corporeal reality, wispy shadows that stalk foggy country lanes in the dead of night. Others understand them to be a metaphysical weight, traces of the past that we carry inside us as we try to make sense of them, whether we succeed in doing so or not.

In ghostlore, an apparition is usually the translucent manifestation of a departed soul. In reality, apparitions can be all the fragments of memory that make up the life you had. In my case, it is the stroke of an eyebrow as I tossed and turned sleeplessly in bed. The damp brush of a coat lapel on my cheek as we waited for the bus. The firm scoop of his right hand as we walked to our local pub.

> 'Whether it's how to tie a shoelace or recalling your first
> day at school, memories make up the autobiographical
> map that helps us navigate the present day.'

My husband wrote these words in May 2017, a little over a year before he died. It was a line that looped in my head on the day I released him into the water. It is a line that I reread on the day I decided to write this book. Every so often, I try to recall the young widow in that rowboat, but, with every month that passes, she drifts a little further with the tide. This widening gap used to panic me, it felt like another loss, until I realised that the oscillating current wasn't pulling her away so much as bringing me closer to a place of transition.

Biologists would call this an ecotone. An area where two different environments overlap. A reed bed that rises above the water level. The gaping mouth of a river where fresh water mixes with the salt of the sea. It would take me some time to find the glade in my grief, a clearing where I could finally consider all the women I've been, and all the women I am. The mute child under the kitchen table. The wistful girl Blu-Tacking Ophelia to her bedroom wall. The hopeful bride in her antique wedding silk. The mangled widow crouched on her bathroom tiles. The go-go dancing reveller on her birthday. Time can distance us from the people we were, but it can't banish them entirely and even if it could, where would they go? On my worst days I wished for it: annihilation, obliteration, total destruction. I pulled down the blinds and I willed the one constant I could feel, the gravitational pull of the earth, to drag me downwards. And it did, for a time, until something began to stir again, my hand reached for a notebook and my words levered me up.

Even when it felt like I was stuck in one place, I was still moving. Imperceptible movements, maybe, but movements nonetheless. On my three-hundred-and-sixty-first day as a widow, I sat perfectly still in a salon chair and looked at my reflection as a pair of glinting scissors snipped away at my hair, large chunks of broken ends that dropped onto my shoulders and scattered onto the floor in damp configurations of dark brown and silver. The hairdryers whirred and an assistant swept away the feathery tips with a broom. It wasn't exactly a radical cut, but it was a determined break nonetheless. A long bob that curved into the curve of my neck. A midway point between my head and my heart.

That afternoon, I walked down streets we previously strolled together and heard a sound in the soles of my feet.

Pa rum, pa rum, it pulsed as my heels carried me home.

Pa rum, pa rum, it throbbed.

A restless rhythm all of its own.

AETHER

18 September 2019

The hillside was on fire. I watched the spiralling embers from the reclining safety of my sun lounger, cupping one hand against my forehead to block out the bright rays of the midday sun. Flecks of charcoal pirouetted around me like burnt confetti in the late summer breeze, sprinkling onto the turquoise water in front of me as the headland smouldered in the distance. It wasn't exactly the poolside vista I had been expecting, but maybe this wasn't so unusual on the north-east coast of Italy at this time of year – although, granted, it certainly looked it. A few flakes settled onto the open page of the book I was reading and I brushed them away with the back of my hand. A billow of thick smoke was now wafting through the olive trees that scattered the rugged coastline from the vantage point of our villa to the cobalt blue streak of the Adriatic Sea only a few miles ahead, and I wondered, somewhat predictably, what the significance of all this was.

Maybe it's just a hillside on fire, an internal voice interjected, *and you should save the introspection for another day.*

I heard the faint sound of drones before I saw the gleaming wings. The garish red and yellow paintwork of a Bombardier 415, a firefighting water bomber that also goes by the nickname 'Super Scooper', which makes a lot of sense when you see it in action. I closed the pages of my novel and watched it circle the scorched land over and over again, marvelling at its graceful loops, following its bulbous nose as it dived downwards into the blue, skimming its surface before soaring back up again, climbing higher and higher until it was ready to deposit its liquid cargo onto the blazing olive groves.

The plane glided through plumes of smoke that moved through the air like paint in a water jar – fattening and bloating, surging and rising, creeping upwards and puffing outwards. It was peculiarly both sluggish and active – a contradiction I recognised only too well as I followed it below with a stillness I was only just beginning to understand. Over the last few months, I had noted my inactivity with increasing frustration, wrestling with what I perceived to be a permanent paralysis, but I was wrong. There was movement there, too; I could feel the vibrations now as I lay lethargically on this blazing hillside. I felt them in the same way you feel your feet throb and tingle after a long walk. It collected in my legs and pulsed around my ankles. There was a tautness between my eyes, and it pulled between my ears, stretching down my spine and branching into my ribs as I lay on the lounger, squinting at smoke plumes.

I looked at the canary plane again. Two commercial flights had jetted above it, airbrushing a giant white X to mark the spot, a meeting of two lines, a point of intersection. I thought about all those tiny people sitting in neat identical rows thousands of miles above me, going somewhere, seeking something, meeting someone, whether through desire or hope or obligation or guilt, and I felt my muscles tighten. As if, if I couldn't move freely with uncorrupted desire, then I'd rather not move at all.

After a year spent in flux, my body was craving an intermission. I hadn't really realised it until I arrived at the tiny medieval village of Montefiore dell'Aso a few days earlier. I was tired and it showed. An hour after my friend Jon, his partner Chris and I arrived at our holiday villa, I opened a cupboard door, reached inside to grab a couple of plates and dropped them with an almighty *crash*.

Tears came and went over the next week with the same intermittent regularity as they had the previous autumn. I walked them into submission, a trick I'd picked up over the last twelve months in a manner, I imagined, not dissimilar to Charlotte Brontë around her family dining table. When my legs stomped at the same pace as my head – through wheat fields and olive groves – those movements seemed to cancel each other out.

One morning I hiked up the road snaking from our guest house over a mountain and through vines, crossed the main road that looped around the hilltop town and shuffled up the stone steps that were carved out of its rocky foundations. The sun beat down on my shoulders and toes, and I bowed my head to give my chest more shade from the wide brim of my woven straw hat. Halfway between the road below and the church spire above, I stopped to take a breath, placing two hands on the wall that separated me from a panoramic patchwork of gold, green and ochre; it seemed as if the trees themselves were quilting the earth together, smoothing over its cracks and crevices.

Looking out over these vineyards, I was transported ten years into the past: to East Sussex on a September morning just like this one. My husband's yellow and orange checked shirt blended harmoniously with the golden grass he stood on, hands in pockets, staring across newly cropped fields towards a giant figure etched into the undulating slopes of Windover Hill. I had never heard of the Long Man of Wilmington, but he had read a lot about this mysterious green giant and was excited to finally pay him a visit. I stood on the road near our parked car and watched him as he followed the chalky white lines with a cupped hand, debating its possible origins.

Like any myth, its unexplained presence is what makes it so intriguing. It was once thought that this 235-foot-tall goliath was cut by monks from a nearby priory and, although for a long time it was believed to have originated in the Iron Age, it is now thought to have been formed from lime mortar in the sixteenth century. One professor hypothesised that it could have been placed on this spot in the South Downs in order to mark the constellation Orion that shimmered above it, and as I looked out across the Italian peaks and ridges, I thought about that cluster of distant stars, hundreds of light years away, burning and pulsating.

The marketplace was quiet, and strolling through its narrow streets I listened to my footfalls as they echoed off the stone walls that fortified this sleepy village. Just me and the masonry. I had left Jon and Chris asleep at the house, bringing only a notepad and pen with me for company, and when I walked into the small cafe where locals came and went, I scribbled down random thoughts as a trio of elderly men, impeccably dressed, chattered away in a faraway language I was content not to understand.

The ancient Greeks looked to the sky to find their quintessence. In Greek mythology, Aether – meaning *always-running throughout eternity* – was the fifth cosmic element, the purest matter breathed by the gods. It was believed that this mystical, luminous material circumnavigated the cosmos, moving in circles, around and around, connecting all things, mortal and celestial, together. A few nights after we arrived at our Italian villa, my friends and I wandered onto the terrace outside, post-dinner cocktails in hand, and looked up into the swathe of midnight blue that sparkled over the opaque sea, its contours only made visible by the soft, mellow moonbeam that dappled across it like a glittering pathway to another realm. With little pollution to cloak the sky, I was astonished by the sheer number of pulsating stars we could see. The tighter I squinted, the more I could make out, my eyes bouncing from one cluster to another, illuminations that beaded the air with pearls.

'Look!' Jon exclaimed, pointing directly above us before reaching for his phone. 'I think that's Cassiopeia.'

I craned my neck as Jon traced a bright *W* with his index finger over the craggy hills, a constellation whose distinct shape is defined by its five brightest stars: Alpha, Beta, Gamma, Delta and Epsilon. When I looked up at these bright globules of hydrogen and helium, I was suddenly struck by the fact that I was gazing at the past. Or maybe the past was gazing at me. Cassiopeia's most brilliant star, Alpha, is roughly 228 light years away from Earth, which means that the light hitting my eyes that evening had taken roughly 228 years to reach them. I thought about these ancient beams of light as I stood there, quietly looking for messages in the sky, words written long ago that might connect me to the watery plumes of my husband's ashes, carried away with the tide, now dancing in the layers of atmosphere above.

Like all good myths, the Greek aether communicated something sacred to me as I took my first tentative steps into my second year of widowhood. This cyclical element represents all the things we cannot see, the stuff that binds us together, from the microscopic atoms that vibrate and rotate to the gravitational waves that squeeze and stretch, and the multifarious emotions that ripple and surge as we go about our daily lives. This aether connected me to my past and present selves, much like the cosmic light in the night sky seemed to dangle a thread from one world into another. Standing under the stars on that September evening, I was reminded of all the connections I had made over the last twelve months, both subtle and seismic, permeations that brought me closer to landscape and language, and to the people I love – my friends, my family and, dare I say, even myself.

My husband's wedding band sits in a small wooden box on my bedroom shelf, next to a ceramic bowl that holds his debit card and passport, dormant objects that still signify something as they sit there soundlessly. Every night when I switch off the light and slide onto my side of the bed, I consider edging inwards, a little closer to the centre, but my body is hesitant to move, and so I remain where I am for now.

Something inside me still wishes to stay.

When I talk of my husband, I often speak of disparate worlds. Mine is inside time, his is supertemporal. I continue to age whilst my husband stays fixed in a past I am drifting further away from with every sentence that I type. And yet, like those luminous balls of plasma in the sky, we are still connected together, for all time is cyclical. I hold the elements within me. Those ashes on my tongue, his embers on the river bed. *My body sings*. What is gained, what is hoped for, and what is lost.

PERMISSIONS

ACKNOWLEDGEMENTS

For my family. My grandmother, who raised my mother with grace and courage. My mother, who taught me that there is no such thing as can't if you have the spirit to persevere and the belief that you can. My father for his unwavering belief in the craft of writing – without which I simply wouldn't be writing today. My sister, Nat, for providing one of the best one-liners in this book. Andy Welch, the gentlest brother I never had. Zoë Beaty, you cradle me, I cradle you, my brightest star. Jonathan King, what can I say? Your hand in mine, it was love at first sight. Cila Warncke, I carry your heart.

With special thanks to my agent, Juliet Pickering, for never letting go. Icon Books for giving me a home. My editor, Kiera Jamison, for handling my words with such precision and perceptiveness. I couldn't have asked for a finer partner – you have made me a better writer. Krissi Murison, for your love and care, and for the nudge I needed at my darkest point.

Richard Ratcliffe and Nazanin Zaghari-Ratcliffe. Hope is the thing with feathers – this book is dedicated to you both.

To the many friends who have carried me through. To name one is to omit another. Forgive me if I avoid a long impersonal list and save my words for when I can squeeze you all after such a long year of separation. I am counting down the days.

And finally, with gratitude to the Wellcome Library, my shelter from the storm.